YOUR
SEVEN-YEAR-
OLD

BOOKS FROM THE GESELL INSTITUTE OF HUMAN DEVELOPMENT

Infant and Child in the Culture of Today
Gesell, Ilg, Ames, and Rodell

The First Five Years of Life
Gesell, Ilg, Ames, and others

The Child from Five to Ten
Gesell, Ilg, Ames, and Bullis

Youth: The Years from Ten to Sixteen
Gesell, Ilg, and Ames

Child Behavior
Ilg, Ames, and Baker

Parents Ask
Ilg and Ames

School Readiness
Ilg, Ames, and others

Is Your Child in the Wrong Grade?
Ames

Stop School Failure
Ames, Gillespie, and Streff

Child Care and Development
Ames

The Guidance Nursery School
Pitcher and Ames

Don't Push Your Preschooler
Ames and Chase

Your One-Year-Old
Ames, Ilg, and Haber

Your Two-Year-Old
Ames and Ilg

Your Three-Year-Old
Ames and Ilg

Your Four-Year-Old
Ames and Ilg

Your Five-Year-Old
Ames and Ilg

Your Six-Year-Old
Ames and Ilg

YOUR SEVEN-YEAR-OLD
Life in a Minor Key

by
Louise Bates Ames
and
Carol Chase Haber

Gesell Institute of Human Development

Illustrated with photographs by Betty David

A DELTA BOOK

Published by
Dell Publishing Co., Inc.
1 Dag Hammarskjold Plaza
New York, New York 10017

For information address: Delacorte Press, New York, New York.

Delta ® TM 755118, Dell Publishing Co., Inc.

ISBN: 0-385-29465-4

Reprinted by arrangement with Delacorte Press

Printed in the United States of America
April 1987

10 9 8 7 6 5 4 3 2 1

To Dr. Frances L. Ilg, who first proposed the concept that every age, like every person, has its own unique individuality.

CONTENTS

YOUR
SEVEN-YEAR-OLD

chapter one
CHARACTERISTICS
OF THE AGE

The Seven-year-old is a very special person and Seven a unique and highly distinctive age. It stands out, coming as it does between the positive vigor of Six and the broad expansiveness of Eight.

Although any Seven, like anybody else, will have his many moments of exuberance, security and happiness, this is in general an age of withdrawal, of pulling in, of calming down. As it begins, parents and teachers may be somewhat relieved. A little calm and quiet is welcome after the tussles and tangles of Six.

But once the child of Seven starts to withdraw, it is almost as though he doesn't know where or when to stop. He goes on and on with his withdrawal until it almost seems that he might be more comfortable and contented if there were actually no other people in the world. Some Six-year-olds seem ready to talk to almost anybody, to share themselves and their ideas and warm emotions. Seven may be much more silent and less giving in company.

People all too often do not behave in a way that satisfies the child of this age, who thinks they are mean, hateful, unfriendly, always picking on him. He thinks his

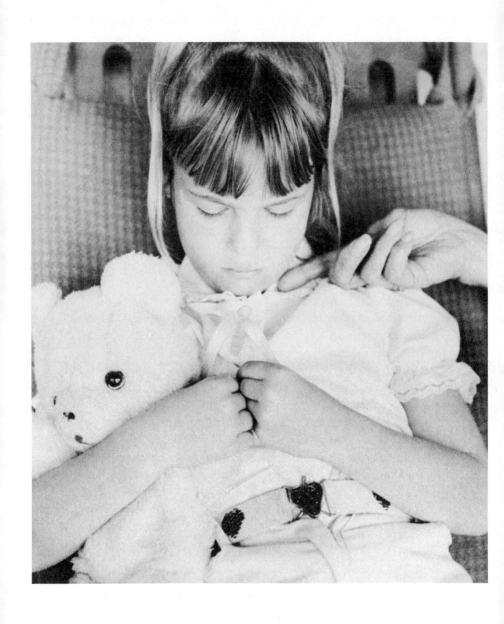

teacher, especially, picks on him, and parents of Seven-year-olds are well advised not to believe all the tales of maltreatment and unfairness that their children may bring home from school.

Seven-year-olds tend to think that people don't like them, or fear that people may not like them: "Of course the kids will make fun of me." The child may often be moody, morose, and melancholy. Above all, the girl or boy of this age is a worrier: worries about everything— the atomic bomb, war, hurricanes, that the family may not have enough money.

Seven worries before second grade begins that it will be too difficult and that the things expected may be too hard. A girl worries that her teacher won't like her; she worries not only about her relationship with others but about herself. Any minor pain or discomfort may be interpreted as a fatal illness. If a boy hiccoughs, he may take it as a sign that he is going to die. He may also worry that others close to him will die.

Yes, indeed, Seven has many worries and also many fears—probably more than at surrounding ages. Sometimes the child is afraid of things that have never happened—of being late for school, for instance. More realistic are such fears as fear of the dark. To him the cellar is full of ominous silences, which he tends to misinterpret. Or he may mistake for a burglar, ghost, or spy the clothes that he hung over a chair when he went to bed.

However, many Sevens have now conquered earlier fears, such as fear of the dentist or of swimming. Also, many are now willing to tackle scary situations, as did the little girl who traveled alone by plane on a summer vacation. Asked if she was frightened, she replied, "Yes, but you have to do scary things if you're going to visit your grandmother." Or a boy may use his flashlight to

dispel frightening shadows in his closet, or get his sister to precede him down the cellar stairs, saying politely, "Ladies first."

In addition to having many worries and fears, the child of this age often feels that he has "all the bad luck." As one girl expressed it, "Why do I always have the bad luck? Why do things so often happen to me? I might as well be dead." The bad luck in this case was that it was time for her to go to bed.

The Seven-year-old also tends to feel strongly that parents like brothers and sisters better than they like him and that they do more for others in the family than they do for him. Typical is the boy whose father fixed an old bike for the boy's Five-year-old brother. The Seven-year-old whined to mother, "He never fixes *my* bike. He never does anything for me. Nobody around here *ever* does anything for me. Nobody cares about me. I might as well be dead." Mother suggested that the boy look in the garage. Maybe Dad *had* fixed his bike. "No," said the boy, "he wouldn't do anything for me. He never does." Actually, the father *had* already fixed the boy's bike as well as his brother's.

Seven's characteristic expression may be a frown, with lips curled downward. Tears come easily, although the child may try to hold them back, because he is embarrassed to cry in front of other people. Also, Seven is easily disappointed. Things so often do not turn out as expected. If things go wrong at play, he is likely to leave the group, mumbling to himself, "I'm quittin'." At home a Seven-year-old boy rushes to his room and slams the door; he may even threaten to run away from home. This is not the expansive exuberance that sometimes drove the Four-year-old out into the world, but is simply a desire to get away from what he may consider an intolerable situation.

Seven is a good listener and, within his own limits, a good student. He likes to read or be read to, watch TV, talk things over, and work things out for himself. A difficult intellectual problem can prove a challenge rather than cause the frustration it might have at Six.

In fact, Seven can be a delightful age if the adult is willing to accept the child's feelings and sensitivities, frequent brooding, and sulking, moodiness, as well as the more pleasant aspects of this quiet, withdrawn age.

To some extent, Seven lives in a world of thought and loves to think things through. Just as his hands are busy touching, exploring, feeling everything with which he comes into contact, so his mind is busy observing, reflecting. He takes in infinitely more than he gives out, and his thought processes are probably much more intense than they may appear to be on the surface. He may even talk to himself in front of the mirror. It is as though the child of this age were trying to define himself, and he does this in part by watching the outside world and then thinking over the things he has observed.

In fact, Seven expresses at times a fine new sense of growing independence, a wish at least to try to work things out without help instead of expecting others to solve his problems for him, as he did earlier. However, for the most part, neither girl nor boy is especially adventurous, preferring to hang on to the old rather than aggressively tackling the new.

Perhaps most helpful to the adult is the child's increasing reasonableness, his willingness (if he is in a good mood) to listen to somebody else's side of the story. Now he can on occasion even lose at a competitive game with-

out blowing up. However, Seven is not an age known for humor. Thus, handling a child through the use of humor may not be as successful as at some other ages.

Intellectually one of Seven's most conspicuous characteristics is a tendency toward perseveration, a tendency to go on and on with a task or situation until it is completed to satisfaction or until somebody stops him. From the adult point of view, Seven is apt to overdo, to go on with one thing too long, such as bounce a ball against the side of the house interminably, or read or watch TV for hours. In fact, parents sometimes comment that it is fortunate that books have chapters and that TV programs have endings. If not, it might be almost impossible to separate child from book or television set. Beginnings may be difficult for Seven-year-olds, but once started, it is hard for them to stop.

The Seven-year-old becomes more aware of himself as a person. He is less *selfish* than at Six, but extremely *self-absorbed.* By absorbing impressions of things seen and heard and read, and by working things over in his mind, Seven seems to be strengthening and building up a sense of self for the time when he will burst out into the world at Eight. The Eight-year-old will take his equipment (his self) out into the world to see what he can do with it. At Seven he is busy improving, strengthening, discovering, his *self.* So time alone with special pursuits is treasured. Seven likes to have a room of his own to which he can retreat and where he can protect his things.

With some Sevens, self-awareness relates strongly to the physical self. Seven is aware of his body and is sensitive about exposing it, especially to the opposite sex; he may refuse to use the toilet at school if there is no door on it; he does not like to be touched.

The typical Seven-year-old has rather high standards

and ideals, is serious about self and is responsible, and wants to do things right. In fact, many mothers feel that their children are too anxious to be perfect, too much afraid of failure. Many Seven-year-olds, girls as well as boys, do set very high standards for themselves, are ashamed of any mistake, and may wish to bring home only papers that are 100's. This wish for perfection may be the reason why, when engaged in desk work, the child erases so much. (Seven has been called by some teachers "the eraser age.") It is hard to get everything *just right.* Seven keeps working at a task until it is finished. Six is an attacker, a good starter. Seven is more of a finisher.

With their characteristic tendency to withdraw, it is not surprising that when things go wrong in their dealings with others, instead of staying and fighting it out as they might have done earlier, Seven-year-olds may merely withdraw from the scene, muttering "Not fair" or "A gyp."

Seven wants to make a place for himself. This place may be a physical one—his place at the table or in the family car. Or he wants to make his place by good or satisfactory behavior, both at home and at school. Sibling difficulties may be a part of his need to make his own place in the family more distinct.

Interest in space may be related to the child's own personal space, either at home or in the world. Seven likes to locate things, especially himself, and wants to know where he stands. His interest in time may also be quite personal. Most Sevens can tell time (they love to have their own wristwatches) and may like to plan their own days. Sevens are aware of the passage of time as one event follows another.

All in all, this is a somewhat sober, thoughtful age.

The calmness and withdrawal and the minor strain that characterize it have their positive as well as their negative sides. Certainly one must notice and admire the child's increasing control—control of body, control of thoughts, control of temper, control of striking out, control of voice. It is small wonder that with all the concentration this control requires, Sevens fatigue easily and must often be protected from their own demands on themselves.

It is useful for adults to keep in mind that the typical Seven-year-old may require more subtle handling than he often gets. He should not be treated like the matter-of-fact creature he may seem to be on the surface. He is most effectively handled if one keeps in mind the subtleties and complications of the feelings that lie just below the surface. While conflict at Six tends to be chiefly with Mother and over things he is supposed to do or not do, conflict now is more within himself, over accomplishments, ability, performance, living up to his own standards.

Although Seven tends to be less happy and satisfied with life than parents may like, good days will steadily increase in number as the child grows older, fatigue will lessen, enthusiasm will increase. The parent of the Seven-year-old needs to steer a delicate course between being reasonably sympathetic to the many complaints that the child may utter and yet not taking these complaints too seriously. The teacher is probably not as unfair as she is reported to be, the other children probably not as nefarious, brothers and sisters not as tricky and mean.

It is important to keep in mind that all this sulking, pouting, and worrying are normal expressions of the age.

The child is not just acting this way "on purpose." Sympathize within reason and at the same time try to remain relatively unmoved. Don't meet dramatics with dramatics.

It was perhaps a superior but certainly not atypical Seven-year-old girl who wrote the following bit of rather *insightful* poetry:

My misery is my mind
And it is my clubhouse too.
And I go up there when I want a hideout
And my little sister comes in my eyes and out my ears
And goes down my misery.

Another more positive but equally characteristic poem was authored by another Seven-year-old:

In the house of civilization
Or in the house of God
Or in the home of home sweet home
In your own house.

I love the house of civilization
I love the house of God
I love the house of home sweet home
in my own house.

WARNING! We must warn readers, as we have done in all our books about what to expect from children at different ages: *Do not take too seriously anything that anybody (we included) tells you about how your child will or may behave.*

Child behavior, for all reasonably normal children, does develop in a relatively patterned way. Stages of equilibrium tend to be followed by stages of disequilibrium, which usually occur before a child can reach a succeeding, and more mature, stage of equilibrium. (See Figure 1.)

And stages or ages of inwardized behavior tend to alternate with stages of outwardized or expansive behavior. (See Figure 2.)

There is even beginning evidence[1] that as the individual develops, stages of rapid brain growth alternate with stages of little or no brain growth, and that stages of little or no growth may correspond with inwardized stages of behavior. There is also a slight possibility that low points in the electroencephalogram pattern may correspond with times of low energy growth and thus with inwardized stages of behavior.

At any rate, that stages of equilibrium and disequilibrium and of inwardized and outwardized behavior will occur as the child matures seems reasonably certain. What we cannot guarantee is exactly when these stages will occur in any individual child. Nor can we guarantee the extent to which either breakup or adjustment—inwardized and outwardized behaviors—will appear. Some children seem always to live a bit on the side of disequilibrium. Even at calm stages or ages, they have trouble with themselves and those around them. Other children, even in the same family, seem always to live on the brighter side of life. Similarly, some children seem always somewhat quiet, self-contained, and aloof; others are nearly always outgoing and expansive.

Each child, of course, has his own personality and individual *sense of self,* depending on many factors: his own basic personality, how the world sees and treats him, as well as how *he* thinks the world sees and treats him. But most children at Seven share the characteristic personality of the Seven-year-old. Although we have not singled

DISEQUILIBRIUM   EQUILIBRIUM

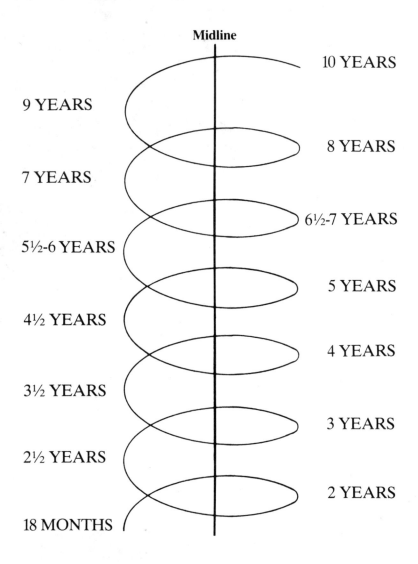

Figure 1
Alternation of Ages of Equilibrium and Disequilibrium

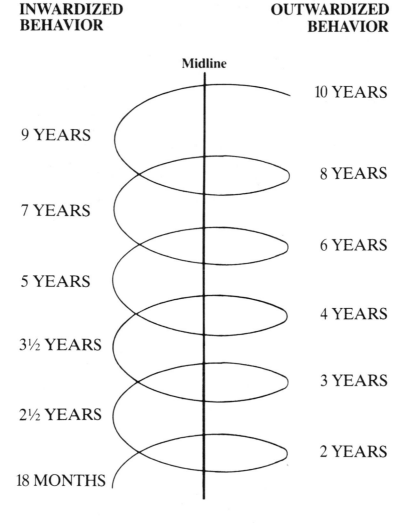

INWARDIZED BEHAVIOR

OUTWARDIZED BEHAVIOR

Midline

10 YEARS

9 YEARS

8 YEARS

7 YEARS

6 YEARS

5 YEARS

4 YEARS

3½ YEARS

3 YEARS

2½ YEARS

2 YEARS

18 MONTHS

Figure 2
Alternation of Ages of Inwardized and Outwardized Behavior

out the self as a special topic, self is really what this chapter is about: what it is like to be a Seven-year-old, in this culture, today.

We tell you about behaviors characteristic of Seven not so that you will check and worry: We tell you what behavior is usually like at this age so that you can, within reason, know what to expect. Then we hope you will *not* worry if your boy or girl changes rather suddenly from outgoing and exuberant to quiet and withdrawn. Each age brings, for many, its own characteristic ways of behaving. Many parents find that the more they know about what to expect, the less they worry when behavior departs substantially from what they may consider the ideal.

chapter two

THE CHILD
AND OTHER PEOPLE

MOTHER

The mother-child relationship is now much less tangled than it may have been at Six, less intense than it will be at Eight. Six, the center of his own universe, tends to take things out on Mother when life goes wrong. Eight's demands of her are often hard to fill.

At Seven, things are more relaxed. Much of the time boy or girl gets on rather well with Mother. The relationship is more companionable and less demanding than earlier. Mothers often say of their Seven-year-olds, "He's better now." This may be due in part to the fact that Mother is beginning to release her child, just as boy or girl is beginning to release her. This reciprocal letting go makes things easier for both. Mother gives fewer commands. Child responds better than earlier to those she does give.

Seven wants and needs his mother to listen to his many complaints, to sympathize with his miseries, to support him when things go wrong, which they often do. He needs her to calm his fears, soothe his anxieties, solve his many real or imagined problems.

17

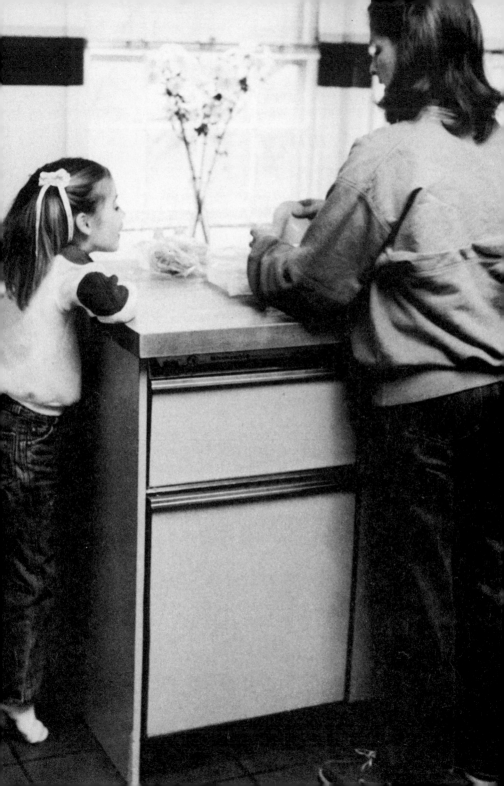

Seven also needs her to argue with: "But, Mommy, why do I have to?" At Six, if things were bad between children and mothers, most children preferred to stay and fight things out on the spot; at Seven they are more likely to walk away muttering "Gyp," "Mean," "Not fair." They may preface their departures with some rude remark, such as "Why should I?" but resistance to commands may not go much further than this. Often the boy or girl merely stays on the spot and looks very, very sad. Seven is sometimes described as self-willed and may indeed get into a real battle of wills with his mother. In fact, there is now and then something almost unchildlike in the force of feelings expressed, not just about tasks to be carried out, but about purely theoretical topics.

Seven's direct relationship with Mother tends to be friendly and forgiving. Most can now (as they may not be able to do at Eight) forgive her a slight mistake. At heart their relationship is a comfortable and sympathetic one and for the most part not overinvolved.

In fact, things tend to be very companionable between them. Seven likes to use the word *we* to refer to Mother and self and enjoys it when they do things together, whether going on an excursion or just having a nice little session in which Mother reads to him. Some Sevens write their mothers very friendly notes expressing a wish for the mother's health and/or happiness.

Some Sevens are extremely proud of their mothers, though self-conscious about them in public, especially if the mothers visit school.

A very special thing at this age is that the child cares what his mother thinks of him. Six cares what she does to or with him. Eight's concern is for what she feels toward him. But at Seven, that thoughtful age, it is her opinion that counts. In fact, many a mother may be surprised to hear son or daughter quoting bits of her advice: "She says 'Be patient' " or "She says 'Don't be too anxious.' "

FATHER

Unfortunately fathers are becoming a rarer commodity today than in the past. Although many of us still take the two-parent family more or less for granted, recent government figures have it that only 80 percent of white children, only 42 percent of black, are actually being brought up in a two-parent home. Even in conventional

two-parent families, commuting fathers may find relatively little time to spend with their children.

This is all to the bad, because as boy or girl grows older, Father is increasingly needed, not to mention appreciated and enjoyed.

Boys for the most part greatly admire their fathers, and some are said to "worship" them. Time with him, especially time alone with him, is greatly treasured, whatever the activity they may be enjoying together. Boys particularly appreciate fathers who will participate with them in any organized sport, such as pitching baseball. They also like to go on long walks with their fathers or share with them such activities as boating or fishing.

Many boys have long, confidential talks with their dads. They relate their worries, problems, and sometimes even their misdeeds. Girls in general tend to have more emotional relationships with their fathers, are extremely sensitive to any reprimand from them, and may even be jealous of Father's attention to Mother.

Both boys and girls tend to seek out their fathers more than their mothers when they need information about things outside the home. This may be especially true in this computer age. If the family does have a home computer, child and father tend to enjoy this new activity. And even before we had computers, many a mother staved off certain difficult questions with "Ask your father," even when she suspected that Father did not know the answer either.

SIBLINGS

Though certainly not past the age of fighting with siblings, Seven fights less than formerly. Girls and boys of

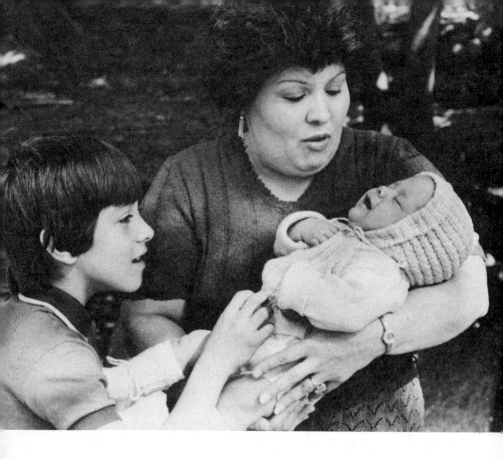

this age are quite as likely to withdraw to their own rooms as they are to stay and fight things out; quite as likely to restrain themselves to muttering and mumbling as to hit and kick.

They are perhaps at their best with baby siblings—two years of age or under. A Seven may actually curl an arm protectively around a little one, who clearly trusts and enjoys such attention from a brother or sister (although a boy who has just hugged and "loved" a Two-year-old may frankly admit—out of her hearing—"I don't really like her. She pinches"). If the young sibling is an infant,

Seven may want to carry her, feed her her bottle, and wheel her in her carriage. But if a younger sibling is closer in age, Seven may tease, bicker, poke, or hit.

The most enthusiasm can be shown for a sibling not yet born. Many Sevens tease their mothers about having a baby or having another baby. However, one such child who had teased unmercifully asked her mother just before the baby came why they were having another baby. "Because you said you wanted one," her mother told her. "Now, whatever made me say a thing like that?" the little girl replied.

Good with much younger siblings, Seven also tends to be good with those considerably older. He admires them, boasts about them, and is gratified when they pay attention to him. In fact, whereas at Five a child often quoted his mother as the authority and at Six his teacher, at Seven he may quote an older sibling.

One of the main problems Seven-year-olds face with siblings near their own age is the fear that these siblings may put something over on them or have more privileges than they. This is a strong age for complaints that things aren't "fair," that the Seven is not getting an equal share of whatever is being distributed.

Sevens are somewhat less likely than Sixes to tattle simply in order to get a sibling in trouble, and fortunately their characteristic absentmindedness often causes them to forget a grudge before they get around to getting even.

A certain unevenness in the Seven-year-old's relationships with his siblings is expressed by parents in such phrases as "Bickers with sister but thinks she's cute," "Protects his sister but teases her." A few are still consistently bad, especially with those near their own age:

"Fight like cats and dogs." However, in general Seven may be the best age yet for brother and sister relationships.

Even when there is considerable physical fighting with siblings, as there may well be, there is possibly a good side to it. As Bank and Kahn[2] have pointed out:

> Aggression, even when painful, represents contact, warmth, another presence. Anyone who has ever observed two brothers wrestling will have noticed that along with pinches and punches there is an enormous

amount of bodily contact . . . The contact that is basic for human survival is immediately available in a near-at-hand and ready-to-fight sibling. . . . Fighting, punching, even drawing blood can help emotionally starved children to know that they are alive, by drawing a reaction from a familiar and intimate enemy. Through pain, the child obtains a rudimentary statement from others: you are alive, you are real, you are being noticed.

We hope that most of your children will receive these messages in less painful ways, but it does seem probable that fighting between siblings must serve some positive purpose.

The inter-sibling behavior we have described is that which takes place in families in which all or most of the siblings are related by blood. It need scarcely be remarked that when the children involved are stepsiblings, bickering, quarreling, and intolerance will in most cases be exaggerated, at least until the new family settles into some semblance of good relationships.

FAMILY

Today families are often different from the way they used to be. Some children have two parents, some only one. Some have stepparents, some adoptive parents. But whatever the family structure, even when it is not an entirely favorable one, most Sevens have strong feelings for their families.

Home and family are very important to Sevens, and the majority are proud of their own families and compare them favorably to the families of other children, even when evidence may be somewhat to the contrary. Most are proud of their parents and their older siblings. Many are quite serious about such concepts as home, family, and even government.

Most are extremely concerned about their place in the family and about their relationships to other members of the family. When things go well, a Seven becomes a real member of the family group, even ready to take on some of the household responsibilities. Many Sevens like to help and often take on certain routine chores, especially on Saturday mornings, when some will empty wastebaskets or garbage pails, cut the lawn, make their beds, tidy up their rooms, help with the dishes, and run errands. (No one child as a rule does all of these things, but any child may do some of them.)

Sometimes this help is spotty. Although he may talk about earning money by helping with chores, the child of this age is not too interested in this. Certainly money does not motivate the way it may at Eight.

Admittedly the Seven-year-old, with his general suspiciousness and paranoia, may insist when things go wrong that he is not really a member of his family—that he has been adopted—and may threaten to run away. But for the most part the child is fond of his family, proud of it, and very protective of his own place in the family.

Most Sevens especially enjoy family outings and as a rule behave better on such outings, and also in public, than when they were younger.

For most, relationships with grandparents continue to be reciprocally warm and admiring, although a child's affection for grandparents may continue to be somewhat

selfish. He likes them, he tells you, because they give him things and take him places. And most children are still quite aware that they can get away with more with their grandparents than with their parents. But a certain appreciation of them as people is often seen. Children show a real love of grandparents for themselves as well as for any practical advantages they offer. And as the children themselves become more thoughtful and increasingly more like adults in word and deed, a new dimension often enters the grandparents' own appreciation of grandchildren.

FRIENDS

Obviously friendship depends on many things other than age—chiefly on any given child's basic individuality, his home, neighborhood, or school, and in some instances sheer luck. Some girls and boys seem never to be without a close friend or group of friends. Others seem to have a hard time finding even a single friend, and if that friend leaves, it may be difficult to replace even that one. But for most, friends are important and conversation may be quite peppered with references to "my friend so and so."

In general, at Seven there is less fighting and squabbling than at Six, although play with even a single friend, let alone with a group, is by no means always harmonious. If things go wrong, as they often do, the child of Seven may characteristically leave the scene instead of staying and fighting it out as he would have done at Six. The fact that Seven is not as aggressively determined to win in any competition or game does tend to make play more harmonious than it was earlier.

While his own success or happiness definitely still comes first, Seven is beginning at least to be aware of his friends' attitudes and reactions. There tends to be less tattling though still considerable concern about the goodness or badness of others.

Several children are likely to gang up against some other child, and many Seven-year-old boys have trouble with older boys who bully them. Group play is not well organized and is still carried out mostly for individual ends. The child may worry about his place in the group and may fear that he cannot hold his own or that others do not like him. He particularly does not want the other kids to laugh at him. There are usually fewer direct physical and verbal attacks on playmates than at Six, although boys indulge in a good deal of half-friendly, half-unfriendly wrestling and scuffling.

It is perhaps helpful, especially when things go wrong with friends, that many Seven-year-olds do not seem to need companionship quite as much as they did at Six, and if friends are lacking, there are many satisfactory and enjoyable things they can do by themselves.

Girl-boy relationships vary tremendously from child

to child. Some boys and girls play together with little regard to sex differences. Some, in leftover Six-year-old fashion, are quite mushy with each other, and there may be considerable talk about love and eventual marriage. One Seven-year-old boy, when asked if he had any special girl friend, asked, "Do I have to name them all?"

Another, asked if his alleged girl friend knew that he liked her, said, "Oh, yes. We give each other stuff and she wrote to me 'I love you.' " Still another reported that when he and the girls played house at recess, "They argue over who's going to be the mother because they all love me and pretend like they're going to marry me one day."

For some, however, discrimination against the opposite sex begins to appear. This is not so much the case with girls as with boys. Some boys just cannot be bothered with girls, and a few are actually hostile, like the Seven-year-old boy who told us of a friend who wore a special cologne that makes girls not like you. (This same boy teased his sister, or so she claimed, by calling her a "naked movie star." He himself denied this accusation by saying, "If I'm *very* angry at her, I might call her 'dummy,' but never 'naked movie star.' ")

TEACHER

Although to many a Six-year-old Teacher's word is *law* and her way of doing things—even though it differs from his parents' way—is the right way, his relationship with her is not as close emotionally as it was in preschool or kindergarten. Nor is it as close as it will be when he turns Seven. Six relates to the teacher through materials and activities—numbers, letters, cutting, pasting.

In contrast, the typical Seven-year-old tends to have a highly personal response to Teacher. Girl or boy may even be said to idolize her and often has a real crush on her. Sevens want their own teacher—no substitutes—and are very demanding of her attention. Many need her permission to begin even the simplest tasks; and will ask "Start here?" or "Begin now?" Much of a child's success and happiness in school depends on the success of his relationship with Teacher.

Children at this age are very personal. There is more of an individual relationship between each child and the teacher than earlier. Children like to stand by the teacher or hold her hand; each child wants a special, separate relationship with her. Children especially like young, attractive teachers who dress nicely. You need a very good teacher for second grade, since she is really paramount for children of this age.

However, as much as a girl or boy may actually like the teacher and depend on her, in true Seven-year-old fashion the child of this age may do a good deal of complaining about her and may say that she is mean and unfair. For the most part this kind of complaint should not be taken too seriously. Also, Seven does not take correction well and is quick to provide an alibi: "That's what I meant" or "I was just going to."

By Eight, many children in school can be controlled by a mere look from the teacher. But now, at Seven, the look needs to be accompanied by words; and if she is standing near the child in question, her influence is even stronger.

Sevens continue to bring things to Teacher, though perhaps not as often as at Six. If gifts seem to the teacher to be of substantial value, it may be wise for her to check their source. (It is not entirely beyond Seven to give the teacher something that actually belongs to his mother.) Children of this age like to bring things from home and like to show the teacher possessions of their own. But Seven is not a good messenger, either for teacher or parent, and should not be counted on to take messages either to or from school.

chapter three
ROUTINES, HEALTH, AND TENSIONAL OUTLETS

EATING

Seven's table manners may not be perfect—a child may still bolt his food, stuff his mouth, and talk with his mouth full—but he is far less likely than at Six to fall out of his chair, and he may not even spill his milk. As one mother put it about her daughter, "She is much less aggravating at the table than she used to be."

With the calm that is characteristic of this age, Seven is able to sit better than earlier and may even show an interest in listening to table conversation and in telling some of his own experiences. Some, however, become almost silent and have less to say than they did a year ago.

Seven is easily distracted by the mention of anything that is going on outside and, if permitted, may frequently pop up from the table to go to the window and check for himself. Children of this age often like to bring to the table something they have just been playing with.

Seven-year-olds still need to be reminded to wash their hands before meals and may resist with "Do I have

to?" Although use of a napkin is sporadic, Seven may sometimes wipe fingers and face inside its folds.

Sevens handle knives, forks, and spoons much better than at Six, and are less likely to eat with their fingers, although they may still use fingers to push food onto their forks.

As for *what* the Seven-year-old will eat, things go better than they did a year earlier. Likes and dislikes may be expressed less vigorously and are accepted better by parents. If a child absolutely dislikes a certain food, often he is not required to eat it. Conversely, some will more or less willingly eat a little of the disliked foods. Some may still dislike strongly flavored cheeses or cooked vegetables. Preference for plain foods remains strong. As one little girl inquired on being shown an elaborate menu in a fancy restaurant, "Don't they have anything *decent* here, like hot dogs and hamburgers?"

As the child reaches the substantial age of Seven, some parents may even feel that he actually has a "good" reason for some of his refusals, whereas earlier many parents felt that they themselves knew best what was good for the child.

SLEEPING

The hour of going to bed moves in on many at seven-thirty or even eight, depending on family custom. (In some families it may be even later than eight.) Many Sevens are able to get ready for bed by themselves and even bathe alone. But most like to have a parent in and out of their bedroom to offer help and a few reminders.

Those who are independent enough to get ready for bed by themselves still want to call to Mother or Father to come and tuck them in and say good night. Some like to chat for a while after lights are out, when they may divulge secrets about what happened at school if the parent promises not to tell the teacher. Many, especially if they have younger siblings, still like to have a bedtime story read to them.

There tend to be two extreme groups of children: those who fall asleep rapidly, and those who lie awake with thoughts going round in their heads. For this second group, sleep is often delayed until nine P.M. or even later while they sing or talk to themselves or listen to their radios. They may listen attentively to catch the conversation of adults or to interpret the sounds of stirrings in the house.

Seven-year-olds have a certain affection for bed. Most are good sleepers, and mothers of such children may report "Sleeps like a log; not even a siren wakes him." Those who fall asleep easily and quickly tend to be the sound sleepers, but they are also often early wakers. They seem to need less sleep than others.

There may be less dreaming at this age than earlier, or at least less reporting of dreams. When he does dream, Seven dreams frequently about himself. He has wonderful dreams in which he flies and floats through the air or dives into the depths of the ocean. Or he may dream of embarrassing situations. Some dream increasingly about other members of the family. Some expand to ghosts and the supernatural or burglars and war, although nightmares in many are decreasing.

A common waking hour is around seven A.M., which may stretch to slightly later on weekend mornings. As a rule, Seven awakens without being called and may even plan to wake up early in order to read or "to have more time." A few are overanxious and get up very early in order not to be late for school.

ELIMINATION

Most children tend to have relatively few problems about toileting. In fact, since retention span is increasing, some even have to be reminded to go to the bathroom before they leave for school in the morning. Fewer children than earlier need to get up at night, and if they do, most take care of themselves completely.

For the majority, bed-wetting is no longer a problem or is only an occasional problem. However, if by Seven a child is still rather consistently wetting his bed, both parents and child are likely to have lost patience with the situation. After checking with a pediatrician to be sure there is no physical problem, many parents like to try one of the good conditioning devices now on the market.*

One other elimination problem at this age may be that some boys and girls are unable to have their bowel movement at school. Fortunately, most can wait until they return home, so few accidents occur.

Most children at this age no longer make silly jokes about elimination functions.

BATHING AND DRESSING

Most Sevens are reasonably good about bathing themselves, although as in other routines they are not self-starters. Thus it may save time if Mother or Father starts the bath.

Once in the tub, most Seven-year-olds enjoy the bathing process even though they are likely to dawdle and get sidetracked or get overly involved with washing one arm or one leg. Many are gratifyingly capable of completing the whole process of bathing; however, many

* Among the best of these devices is U-trol, sold by J. G. Shuman Associates, Box 306, Scotch Plains, New Jersey 07076.

parents do find it wise to check on cleanliness once the child is out of the tub.

As for dressing, preschoolers tend to be proud of any new dressing ability that they may acquire. Fives are relatively capable but often bored, and may need considerable help. Sixes, too, are capable of dressing themselves but often do not want to, and some, especially girls, may have difficulty in deciding what to wear.

Seven is usually past all this, and most boys and girls of this age tend to be rather good and independent dressers, especially once they get started. However, many have a great tendency to be distracted by things in their room or by thoughts in their heads. With one sock on, boy or girl may wander around, asking about telephone wires or how many states there are in the Union. Some can snap to and concentrate by imagining that they are firemen in action. Others are motivated best by direct parental help. If motivation is not provided, parents waste much energy in nagging.

A further difficulty in dressing, besides the need to tuck in loose ends, is the tying of shoelaces. The Seven-year-old is usually quite able to tie shoelaces tight, but often goes around with them untied. It is the old difficulty of "he can but he doesn't." Therefore it is wise to demand a little but not too much. A good plan is to provide long enough shoelaces so that he can tie a double knot.

Many boys and girls at this age are not very interested in clothes. They like to wear old clothes and hate to change to new ones. One boy told us of a friend who wears torn clothes on purpose, although his family has enough money to provide him with good clothes if he wanted them. Very few demand to choose their clothes.

Most accept what their mothers lay out for them. When shopping, most, though not all, will accept what is bought for them without expressing too many opinions of their own.

There is very little interest in the care of clothes. Rips and tears are not reported, and after getting undressed at night, the child is apt to "hang his clothes on the floor." With reminding, girl or boy may pile clothing on a chair.

TENSIONAL OUTLETS

Seven is an age of quieting down, and we see this in the child's tensional outlets. Such outlets tend to be fewer and less active than at Six. While under great stress there may be chorealike total body movements, in general there is less total body wriggling, less kicking at table legs, less swinging of arms, less falling off chairs.

Things may go round and round in the child's mind (a form of tensional outlet), but tensional expression is less visible or audible to others. There is, however, a certain amount of muttering and mumbling, loud breathing, and little throaty sounds. With fatigue the child may pick his nose or bite his nails, even stutter, but there is as a rule much less thumb-sucking. If thumb-sucking does still occur, girl or boy may be willing to make a plan with Mother in order to stop it.

A few children still cling to sleep-inducing stuffed animals at bedtime, but most have given up the favorite blanket.

When tense, Seven does tend to fidget or wiggle a loose tooth. At school the child fingers a pencil, rubs or taps it on his desk, or even jabs it into his desk. Then he

drops it, picks it up, and starts the whole process all over again.

The large amount of erasing that is done at this age may be in part a tensional outlet as well as a wish to get things perfect. Many children whistle or make other noises as they work. Or they may attempt to insert one object into another, manipulating these objects so forcibly that they break. All of this is mostly a matter of hand activity. There is much less facial grimacing, less extension of the tongue, less lip-licking.

HEALTH AND SOMATIC COMPLAINTS

Health, of course, is a highly individual matter, but in general Seven-year-olds tend to be healthier than they were when just a year younger. We don't know for sure why this is so, but since stress as well as contagion brings on illness, we may suppose that second grade is less stressful for many than first grade was. Most children are by now used to the demands of a full day at school, although many seem excessively fatigued at the end of the school day.

In general there are fewer colds, and those that occur tend to be less severe than earlier and less likely to develop complications. There are fewer stomachaches but more headaches. Some of these may be due to visual problems. Certainly there is much eye-rubbing. (Eyewash or eyedrops may make eyes more comfortable, reduce the urge to rub, and thus prevent possible infection.)

In spite of generally improved health, many children complain about their health and worry a lot about it.

Physical hurts invisible to the naked eye are complained about. Children also complain of muscular pains (which are probably real), especially knee pains. Such pains can usually be alleviated by rubbing.

Communicable diseases still strike, but possibly with less frequency than at Six. Clearly children who are members of large families risk more exposure than do only children. But all in all, for many at Seven, less time is lost from school because of illness than at Six, although fevers may occur with any illness.

One special aspect of our culture that has led to improved health for the child of Seven is our growing understanding of the importance of good nutrition. This has resulted in an avoidance of junk foods, artificial colorings and flavorings, and especially foods to which an individual child may be allergic. And although some parents accept a good deal of ill health from a preschooler, by the time the child is Six or Seven, many parents have been exposed to the increasingly impressive literature now available to help them, as Dr. Lendon Smith puts it, "feed your kids right."

chapter four

DISCIPLINE

Quite obviously the most effective discipline is that which is built around the characteristics and nature of the child being disciplined. We know that the typical Seven-year-old is a procrastinator with a very short memory and a tendency to get distracted.

Taking these three traits into consideration, a parent may approach discipline in this way. Suppose your child is watching television and you want him to take out the trash. Clearly he will not relish leaving his program to carry out this uninteresting task. (In fact, whatever they may be doing, many Sevens are not interested in helping around the house.) You warn him in advance: "Just as soon as your program is over, I'd like you to take out the wastebaskets."

But—you can count on it—he will forget your request long before that time comes. So you remind him, "Now that your program is over, how about the trash?" Most, though not all, will comply fairly willingly. Only one last hazard: The child is likely to get sidetracked along the way. Step three is to check to see that this doesn't happen.

It may seem easier to do the work yourself. But most

of us feel that some responsibility around the house is "good for" the child, and this is the way we recommend that a parent go about it. In fact, whatever the situation, Seven needs a lot of reminding, and one of the frequently voiced complaints of the child of this age is "But you didn't remind me!" Six may want and need three chances to do things right. Eight may want only an oblique comment or hint—not "Now wash your hands" but merely "Hands." But Seven likes to be reminded and warned ahead of time, and does best with rather specific instructions.

Though even grown-ups are not entirely immune to the use of special techniques, your typical Seven-year-old is not as vulnerable or responsive to them as he was only a year earlier. Many of your best techniques will simply be ignored. Or the child may turn the tables on you. Six, stubborn and oppositional, will often fall for the simple command "Before I count to ten, I want you to start cleaning up your room." Seven may take over this technique and tell *you,* "Before I count to ten, I want to see a glass of juice on this table."

Thus many parents find that in place of techniques they get the best results if they can establish and maintain a good, responsive relationship with their Sevens. One of the most widely recommended ways of doing this is the so-called "feedback" method. As recommended by psychologist Haim Ginott, this works somewhat as follows.

Your son comes home from school and tells you that all the kids hate him and are mean to him. According to Ginott's original advice, you merely repeat to him what he has said: "Oh, you feel that all the kids hate you and are mean to you."

This rather simple feedback supposedly lets the child know that you are listening to him and that you understand what he is saying. But it has two disadvantages. One is that it sometimes makes the child angry: "That's what I just *said!*" he will tell you. The other is that it is not particularly constructive. Although it shows that you are listening and presumably that you are sympathetic, it does not lead to positive action.

Even sometimes gloomy Seven can be moved to more constructive action or attitude if you handle feedback a little more creatively. You might try "It seems to you that the kids don't like you and are mean to you. What happened?" It may then turn out that some child called him a name. *(Retard* and *gay* are among the more popular epithets this season.) You can then, we hope, work out with him what is the best thing to do when called names.

Sympathetic discussion is nearly always helpful. But it is best to guard against being too sympathetic and agreeing with the child that the teacher is an old meanie or that the other kids are a pretty rotten bunch. As Ginott has emphasized, you don't deny your child's *perceptions:* You accept them as the way things seem to him, but then you try to head him toward more positive perceptions.

Therefore, when your child complains, "You *always* make me do *all* the work around here," when some very simple household task is required, a response such as "Oh, it seems to you that you have to do all the work around here. How can we schedule things to make them fairer?" may get you further than outright denial, a lecture on responsibilities, or a long story about how when you were young you not only walked five miles to school through the snow but did practically all the housework single-handed.

Fortunately, when things go wrong, Seven is more capable of recovery than he was at Six. Now the child can often pull himself together enough to be able to plan how the problem could be solved should a similar situation arise in the future.

Praise, though most children like it, seems somewhat less successful as a motivator at this age than at Six or at Eight. Sometimes you can get a child to do what you want by reminding him of how things seem to other people. There is a certain awareness of others that was definitely missing at Six.

Discipline, as we often emphasize, is not just a matter of punishing for wrongdoing. Discipline ideally involves helping a child to behave in such a way that eventually he will grow to be a self-disciplined, effective, and mature adult. Albert Ellis, in his book *How to Prevent Your Child from Becoming a Neurotic Adult,* gives some suggestions particularly pertinent to this age:

A child can actually become so fearful of failing that he abandons all effort, transferring most of his energy to alibiing. Fortunately there are several things that can be done to help lessen any child's self-defeating achievement needs:

1.   Try to treat your child so that he enjoys many achievements in themselves and not just so that he can win or come out ahead.

2.   Teach your child that real achievement is rarely easy, and that there is nothing disgraceful about taking a long time to perfect any given skill.

3.   Teach your child that perfectionism is great, so long as it relates to performance and not to self. It is all right to try to give a perfect performance. It is impractical to try to be perfect.

4.   Try to help your child perform in a way that he himself finds praiseworthy, not merely to try to perform in a way which he thinks others will praise.

5.   Do your best to see that your child's preferences for great achievements are merely that—preferences and not dire needs.

6.   Teach your child to take his mistakes calmly. He can try to do better next time but should not blame himself for every mistake.

7.   And if you can, try to teach your child to laugh at himself. Help him to get some fun out of others and out of himself as well.[3]

Seven, when given a direction or command, is less likely than Six to refuse outright. Instead of "No, I won't" or "Try and make me," your child is more apt to ask "Why do I have to?"

"Because I say so" may often turn out to be an adequate answer, since Seven is usually asking not so much to find out the reason as simply to stall. However, if you feel that he really wants to know why, tell him. "Why?" is mostly just one of the child's ways of arguing, since Seven loves to argue with adults. "But, Mommy!" is a frequent response. Fortunately at this age most arguments can be settled rather easily. You may not even need to isolate the child (using "Time out" as when he was younger). Sometimes just the mere threat of isolation will suffice, and sometimes just a look from Mom or Dad.

For any communication or request to be effective, your child needs first to hear what you say. Often he really does not hear. Many parents of Sevens suspect deafness. More likely it is mere inattention. Seven lives so deeply within himself that much of the time he tunes out the outside world.

So before you assume that the child has heard you, make sure that this is the case; "Did you hear what I said?" will often reveal that he didn't. For a habitually inattentive girl or boy, try changing your usual approach. Speaking very loudly or very softly sometimes does the trick. Or you may actually need to ring a bell.

Flexibility—now and then giving in—on your part can work wonders. Suppose you've given a routine command to "Be sure to wear your sweater, rubbers, and gloves" and the child comes back with "Why do I have to?" Maybe it really isn't necessary. Perhaps you could, on occasion, say, "Oh, well, maybe you don't need to."

Better still, check yourself before you give too many of these routine orders that come so easily to the lips of the adult. Sometimes, in disciplining, the things we avoid are as important as the things we do. Most specialists recommend that you do not make the same threats over and over. Threats about what you will do "the very next time" something happens, especially if not carried out, tend to fall on deaf ears.

Better to make your rules—for instance that there is to be no hitting—and then when hitting occurs, take whatever disciplinary action you have planned *at once.*

If your own special methods of disciplining your Seven-year-old don't seem to be working too well, you might like to try a currently popular method called behavior modification. One of the best explanations of this method is given by Paul S. Graubard in his practical book *Positive Parenthood.* *

Graubard admits, and most of us agree, that some behavior just cannot be tolerated. He also recognizes that when a child consistently misbehaves, he is trying to tell you something. It's important to listen. Children *need* limits. Without limits, children don't know where they stand.

The most effective and probably easiest way to discourage misbehavior is to let your child know what you expect and then reinforce appropriate behavior.

The four-step method at the heart of behavior modification is: to identify the behavior that is to be discouraged; to intervene in a systematic way; to provide a desired alternative way of behaving; and to evaluate progress by keeping records.

Here are special techniques that may be helpful:

* Paul S. Graubard. *Positive Parenthood.* New York: Bobbs Merrill, 1977, pp. 31–38.

1.   Change the situation *before* the undesirable behavior occurs. Thus if you *know* that your children are going to fight in the half hour before dinner—when they are almost certainly going to be hungry and tired—try giving them a nourishing snack around four-thirty, or feed them before the rest of the family.

2.   Let the child take the consequences of his actions. This idea has been around a long time. (Long ago we heard a little girl pleading with her mother, "Please don't give me the consequences, Mommy.") It is easy to do. Charlie leaves his bike out, contrary to your rules, and it gets stolen. Consequence: Charlie has no bike.

3.   Remove the child from the situation. If your Seven-year-old always fights with his Six-year-old sister about what TV program to watch, don't leave it up to them to decide. *You* work out the schedule of viewing.

4.   If all else fails, a parent can always resort to punishment. Most psychologists urge, and most parents understand, that prevention is better than punishment. However, since most of us are going to do at least some punishing, here are some criteria for using punishment, suggested by Dr. Graubard:

(a)   Ask yourself, is the punishment you are about to give (or have just given) justified? Why do you want to inhibit the behavior in question? Are you trying to impose your will on the child? Is punishment the most effective way to solve the problem? *Punishment is only justified if it is likely to inhibit the problem behavior.*

(b)   Is the punishment immediate? If possible, punishment should immediately and inevitably follow the behavior that you are punishing. This is one of the reasons that "Wait till your father comes home!" is not the best way to handle an unhappy incident that occurs early in the day.

(c)   Is the punishment precise? Punishment, like reward, has to be specific if it is going to work. In other words, is your child certain of what it is he is being punished for?

(d)   Is your punishment effective? If it actually does not inhibit or change undesirable behavior, you obviously aren't accomplishing anything (except, perhaps, relieving your own displeasure).

(e)   Be very sure, if possible, that your punishment fits the crime and is related to it.

Now, if you *are* going to use punishment, keep the following guidelines in mind:

(a)   Use punishment infrequently and make it dramatic but not hysterical.

(b)   Be consistent and systematic.

(c)   After punishing your child, quickly begin reinforcement for alternative and desirable behavior. That is, work on encouraging your child to do something that takes the place of the undesirable behavior. If Susie is always leaving the dishes in the sink when it is her turn to do them, build up a good reward system for her washing them. If quarreling with siblings, especially hitting or pushing them, is the behavior you have been punishing for, build up and reward even short periods when the children play together nicely.[4]

In other words, while prevention is certainly better than punishment, you will at some time or other be punishing your children. So give it a little thought and try to do a good job of it.

And finally, one thing that works to your favor is that at Seven, many children actually want, much of the time, to be good. They are proud if they have had a good day and concerned about bad days. And some are mature enough, on occasion, to take part of the blame when things go wrong at home.

chapter five
GENERAL INTERESTS
AND ABILITIES

PLAY

Your average Seven-year-old is a very busy boy or girl. Play interests are multiple, and playtime—what with school and homework—is short. The fact that the child finds it hard to stop what he is doing, especially if it is pleasurable, tends to make playtime seem all too brief.

Sevens are inclined to be obsessive in their play interests. Many are said to have a "mania" for or a "run" on guns, comic books, coloring. Girls and boys can spend hours at whatever they are doing, whether it is playing the piano, jumping rope, reading, or working at a workbench. Sevens have a greater capacity to play alone than earlier, and therefore can more easily hold to a task.

Children of Seven do not embark on as many new and different ventures as they will at Eight. But most are good at planning what they are going to do. Boys now have some understanding of a model or blueprint. They are inclined to do a little inventing of their own and like to rig up fancy contraptions using cereal boxes or electrical wire. They love to shoot paper airplanes as darts. Girls may be inventive in designing dresses for their pa-

per dolls. In fact, there may be a strong return to coloring and to cutting things out. Some girls cut out paper dolls endlessly.

Both sexes like table games (Parcheesi, dominoes), jigsaw puzzles, or simple card games. They may even tackle a game as complicated as Monopoly. They can handle games better than they did a year ago because it is not quite so vital for them to win. At Six, many just cannot bear to lose and do not do so with any grace. At Seven, they can lose but like to keep on playing until they finally win. At Eight, many can take part in real competition, and can sometimes accept a loss and recognize that an adult opponent may be more skilled than they.

Boys especially love magic and tricks. In some households Sevens spend a great deal of time with computers, at one level or another. They may simply play with children's game computers. Or they may, under adult supervision, play some of the games available on family home computers.

When asked what they like to do best, some Sevens will tell you, "I'm into guns" or "I'm into computers," perhaps in imitation of something they have heard an adult say.

In outdoor play, Seven exhibits extremes. Sometimes he is tearing around, tossing a handmade paper airplane; at other times he is content to hang around, talking, swapping cards, or playing house.

Boys especially are interested in acquiring the ability to use a bow and arrow and to bat a ball. Both of these skills require a new orientation to the side position. Carpentry is a favorite occupation, and Seven likes the tug and pull as he saws a board. Kite-flying requires a certain skill. Girls are busy jumping rope, playing hopscotch, and roller-skating, and some, like the boys, are interested in playing ball.

Collecting is very important, and collecting interests may range from bottle tops to stones. But quantity, rather than quality or classification, is the rule. If asked what kind of stones they collect, those children who collect stones will tell you, "Oh, just any kind." It is very touching to see a little boy walking along the beach, filling a bag with "any kind" of stones. (Stones for many do seem to exert a tremendous fascination. One girl we know gave her father her favorite stone, carefully gift-wrapped for his birthday. Another sent her grandmother a box of stones as a present.)

Not only stones but all aspects of nature are of extreme interest to many children of Seven. Whether inanimate (stones, sand), animate but relatively immobile (grasses and trees in fields, parks, and woods), or living and moving (birds and butterflies or one's own pets), all provide real fascination to a boy or girl of this age. "The thing I like best in the whole world is nature," confided a Seven-year-old Australian girl when asked what she enjoyed most. Some like to build, and play in, tree houses.

Group play is similar to that at Six, although now

there is more demand for "real" paraphernalia. Playing house may have stronger personal than practical content, but when they are playing library, for example, children want "real" library slips and want to go through the whole formal process of signing books in and out. A boy may equip his tent with a cot, table, and chair, writing material, and a toy gun. (Regardless of how adults may feel about them, boys at this age do love to play with guns.) In playing house, some really seem to feel that they *are* the role they are playing—mother, father, baby —and may even feel that they *are* naughty when they are playing the bad child. A teacher may be surprised to hear her tones imitated as the children play school.

Play is more complex now than it used to be, because children can take and give instructions to each other on how the roles should be played. At Six, each wanted to do things his own way and there was much less coopera- tion.

Ball play is very big with many at this age. They are very serious and sincere about it, especially when it is a structured game (under the supervision of adults). Many are quite awed by the coach. They are also delighted if their father will drive them to and from the playing field. They very much like to have at least one parent watch their games.

Some now enjoy soccer, although perhaps the most popular form of organized ball is baseball.

READING

The typical Seven-year-old is in a transition stage when it comes to reading. He still likes to be read to, but

at the same time, especially as the year moves on, he likes very much to read by himself.

Many Sevens are already fair readers, and reading may be one of their favorite activities. Nearly all can get the sense of a story, even without knowing all the words. Some at this age are known as "chain readers," for they move almost without pause from one book to the next.

Topics most enjoyed vary tremendously from child to child, but it seems safe to say that for nearly all, riddles and "knock-knock" books are surefire favorites. The Six-year-old wants a grown-up to know the answer to his riddles. Seven finds it amusing if an adult guesses wrong. Eight *wants* the adult to get the answer wrong.

Humor in general is not well developed at Seven years of age. The Seven-year-old can smile and laugh with the best of them, but spontaneous humor is not his strong suit. However, the intellectual amusement offered by riddles is almost universally appealing at this age, and this shift from the often rather silly giggling of Six marks a big step in maturity.

Some Sevens will still listen with interest if Mother is reading preschool-type books to younger siblings, but for their own reading, these are usually not the books of their choice. The child of this age is more likely to prefer the "I Can Read" books put out for beginning readers by several of the major publishing companies.

Some are still very interested in dinosaurs, as earlier, but many have moved on to a love of magic or of fairy stories. They especially like the parts about magic in these stories, especially when it is used to punish wicked characters. Boys are especially interested in sports, war stories (books of the *Star Wars* variety are currently popular), stories about airplanes and space in general, electricity, earth, and nature. Many girls share these interests (television has been a great leveler), but girls probably more than boys like fairy stories and stories about relationships between people. Boys rather more than girls enjoy violence in their stories.

Now that most can read, Sevens become aware of comic books. Not as popular as they may be later, comics are nevertheless great favorites with many. Preferences vary, although the *Garfield* type of humor is extremely popular. Some children love to read their favorite comic strips in the daily paper.

MUSIC, RADIO, AND TELEVISION

Seven often expresses a strong desire to take piano lessons. This enthusiasm about the piano may not last, but if a parent can try it as a temporary experiment, it can be all to the good.

Although some children may like to carry around a little transistor radio, for most, television largely takes the place of radio. It is now a part of the daily routine, and children very much dislike missing their own special programs. The amount of watching, as well as the type of programs watched, may have to be restricted by parents.

Many Sevens are still stuck at the cartoon level. They still enjoy such cartoons as *Scooby-Doo, The Unicorn, Mickey Mouse, The Flintstones, Superman, Star Wars,* and *The Empire Strikes Back.* Some move up a step from cartoons to such programs as *Nickelodeon.* If they have cable, they may watch the Disney channel. But unless encouraged by an adult, the ordinary Seven-year-old does not as yet exhibit very sophisticated television taste, much as he enjoys the medium.

Interest in movies is variable but nowhere near as great as it was in the days before TV. If children do go to the movies, they mostly prefer musicals and animal stories or perhaps Westerns. Most *hate* love stories.

CREATIVITY

Creativity is a quality that varies perhaps more than any other from child to child. Native ability—of child and of parent—seems to influence its expression rather more than the age of the child. There are creative parents and uncreative parents, creative children and uncreative. In some families not only potholders but even home-made pots abound. In other families creative expression tends to be more verbal than manual. Some children paint; some children, even at Seven, play musical instruments. Others talk or write. Others are creative in their interpersonal relationships.

Unless truly gifted, even a moderately creative child may slow down a bit in his artistic expressions at the age of Seven. Certainly fewer large, messy bits of artwork are brought home from school. The house is less cluttered with drawings and other artifacts that must be carefully saved and treasured. Also, since creativity requires change and willingness and ability to do things differently, Seven's tendency to persevere and perfect may work against any large measure of creativity.

It seems safe to say that although a truly creative child may show this ability at almost any age, Seven itself may not be a particularly creative age.

THE CHILD'S BODY IN ACTION

The average Seven-year-old seems much better coordinated physically than he was just a year earlier. He no longer trips over a piece of string or bumps into things. His arm and leg movements are less far-flung. Seven, whether boy or girl, is now more self-contained, more restrained, more cautious, and less interested in sheer physical activity for its own sake. He also shows a new awareness of heights and is now somewhat more careful when climbing or playing in a tree.

Seven's posture is more tense and unilateral than it was just earlier. Thus, when working at his desk, he often leans to one side, over his nondominant arm, face almost down on his desk. He can maintain one posture for a long time. The child of this age is precise, compact, direct, pulled rather neatly together. At home a favorite posture is lying prone on the floor, resting on one elbow, and activating legs while reading, writing, or working.

In gross motor activities, Seven is fairly cautious but not fearful. In ball play, most boys are better at batting than at catching. The side stance of bow-and-arrow play and the cautious release of the arrow have a special appeal. Seven is developing the physical stamina to hold up better during the winter season and is therefore beginning to enjoy skiing, sledding and skating.

Visually, Seven is a more focal and pulled-in age than Six. The child tends to draw near to things he can't see well. He may pull the things up close to him or may lean over close to the thing he is viewing. He also tends to restrict himself visually, choosing a smaller unit than formerly in order to comprehend it. He almost seems to absorb into his very self the things he looks at.

Children of this age become extremely engrossed in what they are doing. They are still apt to touch and manipulate anything that catches their eye. One eye leads, but the partner eye participates; improving binocularity is in evidence.

Seven is much less distracted by peripheral movement than at Six. Unawareness of things on the periphery of vision may result in eye injuries when the child runs into things he has not noticed.

Because of his difficulty in shifting his vision from near to far, the Seven-year-old should either work at the blackboard or at his seat; he should not be required to sit at his desk and copy from the blackboard. Seven's eyes tire easily, so he needs to avoid staying too long at one task.

Teething which has been active in the past years, in most Seven-year-olds has come a long way. By Six years of age lower central incisors and six-year molars have erupted in the average boy or girl. By Six-and-a-half the upper central incisors and lower lateral incisors have erupted in the majority. Upper lateral incisors come in at Seven, although it is not until Eight for most that one can anticipate a full complement of four six-year molars and all four upper and lower incisors.

chapter six

THE CHILD'S MIND

Scholars have long argued about the relationship between mind and body. Are they two quite separate entities, as some contend, or are they for all practical purposes one and the same? Is bodily activity, like thinking and talking, just one *aspect* of the mind in action?

An increasing number of people nowadays seem to agree with us and with that well-known student of child behavior Dr. Arnold Gesell in maintaining that mind and body are not two separate entities but rather that mind expresses itself in nearly everything the person does, from earliest infancy onward.

We ourselves hold with Gesell that mind manifests itself. It manifests itself in almost everything a person does. A child's motor behavior—for instance his ball throwing—can be as much an example of his mind and body at work as are the things he says. Even the major personality changes that occur as the child grows older—the pulling in that occurs so conspicuously at Seven years of age, for example—are demonstrations and expressions of the mind in action.

In this chapter we present special information about time and space; reading, writing, and arithmetic; language and thought; death and Deity; the child's ethical sense and his understanding about sex. We give this information as a separate chapter simply because, to many people, talking and thinking seem different in character from such other behaviors as eating, sleeping, ball-playing, and socializing. They seem different and somehow special. Actually, in certain ways, talking is not all that different from such a behavior as tree-climbing. In both, the brain directs some special parts of the body to behave in special ways.

The mind is not just a separate something at the top of one's head, occupied exclusively with talking and so-called thinking, or, to use a currently popular term, cognitive behavior.

SENSE OF TIME

There is a big jump here, both in interest and ability. Sixes cannot, as a rule, tell time by the clock. Most Sevens can tell what time it is—not only what hour but how many minutes past or before the hour. Most know how many minutes in an hour. Many at this age are very anxious to have wristwatches of their own.

The child can usually tell what month, what day of the month, and what season it is. He also knows the month and day of his birth.

There is an increasing understanding of and appreciation for the duration of time, although with his characteristic tendency to dawdle Seven may delay almost up to a deadline and then finish with a spurt.

Many at this age are extremely worried, often beyond reason, that they will be late for school. If your child expresses this kind of anxiety, your best bet is to go over with him that you will call him in the morning in plenty of time, that his clothes will be laid out for him (if this is still necessary), that breakfast will be ready. That is all *you* can do. How he feels about it is up to him.

Seven likes to plan his day as well as know the sequence of the months and seasons. Often he will ask how long before his birthday or Christmas. One Seven-year-old who was thinking ahead to the time when she would be Sixteen remarked, "It's a long time to wait. Nine years. Even one year is a long time."

The customary phrase "I forgot" also suggests Seven's special interest in time, implying as it does that "I *did* know a little while ago, even though I don't know now."

SENSE OF SPACE

Seven is not an expansive age, but boy or girl is reasonably well oriented in home, school, church, and neighborhood. Community interests now include details about stores of various kinds (especially the convenience store where spare cash is spent), the police station, the firehouse, and the hospital.

Children nowadays are of course much more interested in space travel than children used to be, although actually many are quite blasé about it. But in school many are still not ready for the study of faraway times or places. Some are trying to orient themselves in the world, such as the girl who asked, "How old was I before I realized there were other places besides right here?"

Seven is especially interested in various objects in space—the earth's crust, heat, fire, sun, stones. Girl or boy may also be interested in water in all its forms: waterfalls, streams, oceans. Some like to dig wells or try to dig their way to China.

READING

Reading in most has improved tremendously during the last year, often to the extent that many read to themselves silently for pleasure. In school the child likes to know how far to read and may be most comfortable if allowed to use a marker. At home many will read as long as permitted.

In general, Sevens recognize most familiar words quickly and accurately. Their approach is still somewhat mechanical and they do make certain errors. Thus they may not pause at the end of a sentence or paragraph. And they may omit or add such familiar simple words as *and, he, had,* and *but,* or a final *s* or *y.*

Seven hesitates on new words and prefers to have them supplied (rather than be forced to spell them out), since he does not like to interrupt the flow of his reading. Or he may simply guess, using a word of similar appearance, often one with the same first and last letter, although the length of the word may be shortened *(green* for *garden, betful* for *beautiful).* Also, substitutions of meaning *(the* for *a, was* for *lived)* are prevalent. Vowel errors *(pass* for *puss, some* for *same)* are also common. Speed of reading, like fluency, shows marked individual variation.

Inevitably some Seven-year-olds have not actually reached a full Seven-year-old level of reading. Many are between what reading specialist Jeanne S. Chall calls stage 1 (initial reading or decoding, ages Six to Seven), and stage 2 (confirmation, fluency, ungluing from print, ages Seven to Eight). In the first of these stages, according to Chall,

70

the child learns the arbitrary set of letters, and associates them with the corresponding parts of spoken words. He interiorizes cognitive knowledge about reading, such as what the letters are for, and how to know when a mistake is made.

In the second stage,

the child consolidates what was learned in stage 1, and reading increases in fluency. In this stage reading is still not as much for gaining new information as for confirming what is already known to the reader.[5]

The typical Seven-year-old, though not as competitively motivated as at Six, likes to do things right, likes to succeed, likes to complete a task undertaken, and is glad to please parent or other instructor. Thus, when help is needed with reading, the child is a little more receptive to necessary correction and criticism than at earlier ages. Instead of growing angry and getting into a fight, as he might have done at Six, chances are he will accept a correction and try again. His natural persistence will now stand him in good stead.

If the Seven-year-old is getting too mixed up, Mother may be wise to stop a reading session and take it up again some other time. And Seven's fatigability must be kept in mind. Since Sevens do not always protect themselves from overdemand, the person helping them may have to provide the necessary protection.

Seven's ability to spell usually lags considerably behind his ability to read. He enjoys copying words but still cannot spell them by heart; he becomes especially confused over vowels. *I* seems to be his favorite vowel

and the one substituted most often, e.g., *sit* for *sat*. He·
also substitutes it as he pronounces words—*cin* for *can*,
tin for *ten*.

PRINTING AND WRITING

While most children are not ready for cursive writing
until they are Eight, the average Seven-year-old has
come a long way in his printing skills. In printing, Seven
has gone so far as to be interested in comparative size,
and the height of capital and small letters is becoming
more uniform, although they may get larger as the writing proceeds across a page.

Even at Six most children can print their full names.
By Seven this ability is practically universal. Reversals
and substitutions of letters are for the most part a thing
of the past. In general, when printing names, capitals and
small letters are not confused, letters are of more or less
even size, and there is good spacing between first and last
names. Girls tend to be ahead of boys in evenness of size
of letters and evenness of baseline.

As a rule, a Seven-year-old cannot write his address,
in fact may not even know the meaning of the word. But
if you ask where he lives, he can tell you. This does not
mean that he can write (print) his address; for most, this
ability does not come until Eight years of age.

Most can now name the day's date, but only about a
third of Sevens can write it.

As far as numbers are concerned, most Sevens can
form their numbers up to 20 or beyond. Numerals tend
to be even in size, and for the first time the baseline is
even. There are far fewer reversals, either in the shapes
of single numbers or in the order of numbers in the

teens. (They no longer write 31 for 13, for example.) And they no longer write the 2, 3, 4, etc., before they write the 1.

Seven is making his numbers smaller now than he did at an earlier age (approximately a quarter of an inch) and of more or less even size. Spacing has been reasonably good for the past year.

Pencils are tightly gripped, though less so than at Six, and are held close to the point. Grasp, though tight, tends to loosen suddenly, so that the child is apt to drop his pencil repeatedly while working. Seven is very fond of pencils. The favorite Christmas present of a Seven-year-old friend of ours turned out to be a box of pencils. He opened it with rapture, exclaiming, "Pencils!" And then when he saw that they were personalized, he shouted, "With my *name* on them!"

ARITHMETIC

Counting: Most Seven-year-olds can count to one hundred by ones, fives, and tens; they can count by twos to twenty.

Naming coins: Seven-year-olds can name penny, nickel, dime, quarter, half-dollar, and they can tell how many pennies go into each.

Addition: Sevens are usually correct within twenty. A few make errors of plus or minus one, suggesting that they are still counting one by one. Others know combinations, especially the even combinations (such as 3 + 3) by heart, and break harder ones down into known combinations and figure from there.

Subtraction: Sevens can subtract correctly within ten.

They count backward from the larger number or use balanced numbers; they know many combinations by heart.

When doing written work, Sevens do not shift easily from addition to subtraction on the same paper. They like either to add or subtract but not to switch from one process to the other.

Simple fractions: They learn these by dividing up all kinds of real things into halves, quarters and three-quarters. They know that there are five pennies in a nickel, four quarters in a dollar.

Numbers in order up to one hundred: Most understand place value in number notation, and the fact that each of the 4's in 444 has a value that depends on its place.

Size and shape: They understand both size and shape, including some simple proportions, such as four times as heavy, twice as tall, nearly as old. Seven likes to play with shapes and to copy patterns.

Of course, all of these are generalities. It is quite as important to try to understand the individual Seven-year-old's math process as to know what the average child of this age can do. Some children guess and tend to be surprisingly good guessers. If they do make an error, it may be merely plus or minus one. Others, when given a simple oral arithmetic problem, immobilize their heads, their eyes shooting upward laterally and obliquely as they think. When asked how they arrived at their answers, some say "I used my head." Others may find it difficult to explain how they figured things out. Thus one boy, when asked by his mother to add nine and six, counted "One, two, three, four, five, six, seven, eight, nine;" then clapped his hands over his eyes and apparently went through considerable mental torture. He came out with the correct answer, fifteen. Asked how he got it, he said, "I count to nine. Then I have to think. I can't think good with my eyes open, so I close them and *think like anything.*"

This same boy was getting his subtraction all wrong and suddenly began to get it right. When asked about the change, he said that at first he didn't know what he was supposed to do, so he just put down any old number. But when he found out how one did it, he could do it all right. Others start out all right, but before they complete a problem they tend to forget the process.

LANGUAGE AND THOUGHT

"Mind manifests itself in virtually every behavior" was a favorite saying of the late Arnold Gesell. Unlike Piaget, he did not restrict so-called mental or cognitive abilities to things that could be expressed verbally.

Since Seven is above all a thoughtful age, at no time in the child's life, perhaps, do we see the mind at work in all aspects of living more than at this inwardized, serious period. Nearly all the behaviors described in this book are, in our opinion, expressions of the mind at work.

We note an increasing precision in *language* itself. The child of Seven tries to say things just right. In telling about some kind thing a person has done for her, a girl will say "That was nice." She then amends this to "It was *very* nice." Seven also wants others to say things just right. If an adult, going by a Christmas display, should remark "Look at all those wise men," the Seven-year-old will correct this loose statement with "There are only three."

At this age there is also an expanded use of adverbs. Seven livens his conversation with such words as *fright-*

eningly, surprisingly, disappointingly, and *remarkably.* Or he may employ such mature expressions as "That embarrasses me" or "I feel embarrassed." *Serious* is a frequently used word. A Seven-year-old of our acquaintance told his visiting grandmother "This is serious. Daddy is allergic to cats and we have a mouse in the cellar."

There is a somewhat negative tone to much verbalization at this age, strong use of the word *can't:* "I can't," "I can't figure it out," "I can't think," "I can't get it," or "Suppose I can't remember?"

Sevens also have many verbal ways of refusing or delaying a situation: "I haven't had that," "I've never done that," "I never heard of that," "I don't feel like it." Or: "I got to think it over," "I was just trying to think," "Oh, wait a minute."

And there is much criticism of their own performance: "What's the matter with me?" "What was that supposed to be?" "Crooked," "Can't make it straight," "This is terrible," "I can't do it good." The child is beginning to seek praise, which is increasingly the case at Eight, by disparaging his own products: "That isn't very good, is it?" "I made it but it's terrible."

It is fair to say that much of the child's language is used complainingly. As mentioned earlier, he complains a great deal that people don't like him, that they are mean and unfair, that there is nobody to play with.

Sevens are interested in the meanings and spellings of words and like to use pictorial dictionaries. They are able to give the similarities between two objects. They now relate thinking to the head or mind: "You have to think it up in your head" or "It went out of my mind." The child uses language not only in face-to-face situations but also in the social telephoning with friends that has begun.

As to what Seven-year-olds think about such basic concepts as death, the Deity, and that important holiday Christmas, we have found the following:

In families that are strongly churchgoing, many children still believe firmly and without question what they have been taught. They do not question the reality of the Deity and believe that when you die "your body goes into the ground and your soul goes up to heaven." Some Sevens, with their increasing interest in family relationships, are getting the idea that as a rule the oldest people in the family die first. Thus, just as grandparents may have died, later parents may die and finally the child himself will die. Some deny the possibility of their own deaths, although one Seven-year-old told us recently, "It's all right with me."

Many Six-year-olds seem extremely afraid that their mothers will die. Seven, for all his other worries and anxieties, seems less concerned about this.

Although some Sevens do seem rather casual about death, others show a marked interest in its causes: old age, violence, disease. They also show marked interest in coffins, burial rites, and cemeteries.

In families in which religious interest is not strong, some children express a certain skepticism and begin to distinguish between what they "know" from what they have been told. As one little boy put it, "I have never seen God!" A child may ask, "How did God get up into heaven?" or "How can He see everything and be everywhere all at one time?"

Christmas still means a great deal to most. Seven has very definite ideas about what he wants as gifts and tends to be extremely disappointed if he doesn't get them. Belief in Santa Claus varies from child to child. Most have at least an inkling that he may not exist, but most do not want to be told this as a fact. Many still leave out cookies and milk, just in case he does show up.

As for *thinking,* in the way in which the Swiss psychologist Piaget uses the term,[6] many Sevens are emerging from what he calls the preoperational stage. According to Piaget, this stage predominates from Two to Seven years. The child then moves into a stage that Piaget calls concrete operational, which starts around Seven and continues up to Eleven. By Piaget's definition, at the preoperational stage the child is still the center of the world and everything that moves is alive. The child is apt to explain events in terms of his own needs and wishes: "It rained because I wanted it to." He also believes that objects and natural events have human thoughts and feelings: "It rained because the cloud was angry." And the child often explains things in terms of magic.

In the concrete operational stage, which begins around Seven, children see the ways in which objects can be alike but also different. They know that the shape of a container does not affect the quantity it holds. They also understand the idea of numbers and can tell that ten marbles in a row is more than eight in a row, even if the rows are the same length.

Although Piaget does not place the beginnings of abstract thought until Eleven or Twelve years of age, we and others do feel that many Seven-year-olds are capable of at least a certain amount of abstract thinking.

ETHICAL SENSE

Seven is a good little fellow. Not yet perfect, he has very definite ethical standards and tries hard to live up to them. He is proud of his "good" days and worries about his "bad" ones.

The Seven-year-old is quite conscientious about not taking things that belong to others, although some do lapse. He tries to tell the truth. Seven is definitely concerned about the wrongness of lying and cheating, especially in others. He is somewhat less likely to blame others for his own misdeeds than earlier, but is quick to tattle about any breach of the ethical code on the part of siblings and friends. If he himself missteps, he is very ready with an alibi: "I didn't mean to," "I forgot," "I was just going to do it," "That's what I meant."

Fairness is now very important to the child. Some seem to be aware of a force outside their own control that they

call "fairness" or "luck." When in trouble, Seven is apt
to complain "That's not fair." It is still hard for others to
change his mind, but he may listen to reason and reluc-
tantly agree to go along with another person. Sevens do
have standards and try to live up to them, and thus can
be appealed to ethically at least part of the time.

Seven's idea of good and bad is beginning to be
slightly abstract. It is no longer concerned solely with
specific actions allowed or forbidden by parents, but involves the beginnings of a generalized notion of goodness and badness. One Seven-year-old girl dictated a list
of all the things she had done that day "thinking about
myself" (i.e., out of selfishness) and "thinking about
others" (out of unselfishness).

THINKING ABOUT MYSELF

1. Eating omelet with my fingers.
2. Saying "Waah!"
3. Speaking rudely to my mother: "Yes you will!"
4. Contradicting.
5. Not washing hands before playing the piano.

THINKING ABOUT OTHERS

1. Obeying my mother, picking up the living room.
2. Went to bed willingly, fell asleep quickly.
3. Remembered to close the door to keep the bathroom warm.
4. Didn't shout in the library.

5. Came off the ice quickly when Anne came for me.
6. Put my glasses away in their case.
7. Put my glasses on when I'm reading.
8. Dressed quickly without dawdling.
9. Looked before I crossed the street.

Seven has an increasing sense of possession and does a better job than earlier of taking care of possessions. He may even help clean up his room. The child's feeling of possession now definitely extends to school things. He likes to have a schoolbag that contains his own pencils, eraser, and whatever else he needs. There is considerable interest in swapping things with others, although this tends to be more at an "even swap" level than involve any actual bartering.

There is at this age an increasing interest in money, and while money seems to burn a hole in the pockets of some, others are interested in saving at least some of their money. A few are ready for an allowance.

SEX

What with television and the increasingly frank and detailed books now available for the young, Seven-year-old boys and girls tend to be better informed about sexual matters than they used to be. But regardless of exposure to pictures and print, understanding takes time. There are still many Sevens—at least those who grow up in a fairly protected atmosphere—who do not understand or are not interested in the details of intercourse. Many are quite satisfied with the notion that two seeds (or eggs), one from the mother and one from the father,

come together to start a baby. They are not yet concerned about how the seed from the father got into the
mother.

However, there is now an increasing interest in babies,
and most know that the baby grows inside the mother.
They may ask how Mother knows there is a baby inside
her, how long it takes for a baby to be ready to be born,
how the baby gets out, and especially how much it will
cost. One boy, when told the approximate figure, remarked in shocked surprise, "I don't understand that at
all. A baby grows inside you, doesn't it?"

Pregnancy tends to be more interesting to the child of
this age than it used to be. He may ask his mother very
early in the pregnancy "What's the matter with you?
You don't act the same." As the pregnancy proceeds he
may like to feel the baby kicking against his mother's
abdomen. Most Sevens know that a woman can have
more than one baby and that much older women do not
have them. Many are interested in details of their own
births.

Some parents note that as the child moves on from Six
to Seven, sexual curiosity becomes more disguised and
less outspoken, and any sexual behavior begins to be
hidden, even in a relatively permissive environment.
There is probably considerably more interest and even
activity than those who emphasize the so-called latency
period believe, but most Sevens do seem to question less
about sex than they did a year earlier.

Although the amount of sex play varies a good deal
from child to child, and a highly sexed child or one
whose friends are active in sex play may indeed indulge,
for many there is less overt sex play than at Six. In fact,
at Seven many are becoming self-conscious about un-

dressing or using the bathroom in the presence of younger siblings of the opposite sex. (As one little girl put it to her brother, "People like their privacy, you know.") Also, name-calling involving elimination words or sex terms tends to fall off considerably, although some may still use such expressions as "You old penis butt."

PROJECTIVE TECHNIQUES

One special way psychologists have of measuring a child's mind is through the use of what we call projective techniques. A projective technique is a kind of test to which there are no right or wrong responses. Rather, the child or adult projects his personality or way of thinking and experiencing onto what may be considered a rather fluid medium.

One of the best known of these techniques is the Rorschach inkblot test.[7] In giving this test, we show the child a series of cards, on each of which is printed a more or less shapeless inkblot. Some of the blots are colored, some black and white. We ask the child to tell us what the blots look like to him. From what he says, we believe we can tell a good deal about what he is like and what the world seems like to him.

Not only do different children see different things, but in general, different kinds of things are seen at different ages. Thus the personality characteristics of any given age seem to make themselves evident in the child's responses to the inkblots.

The typical response at Seven seems to confirm what we have observed in more homespun ways. It suggests a love of the horrible and violent. It suggests that just as the Seven-year-old at home or at play may prefer the morbid and melancholy to the cheerful and happy, so in responding to the relatively neutral Rorschach blots he quite typically sees murdered people, people being hurt and screeching with pain, poisonous spiders, dripping blood, dead bats.

Such typical responses lead us to believe that it is not just the environment—the radio, television, movies, and comic books—that give Seven his lust for gore, his love of the horrible. We suspect that these preferences may be a normal expression of the child's way of seeing life at this age.

chapter seven
SCHOOL

On the whole, Seven accepts the return to school in the fall without protest but may anticipate that second grade will be "too hard." If the first-grade group is able to make a few advance visits (such as going to a play or picnic at the end of the year) to the second grade, this can help to forestall and alleviate such fear.

The child's success or failure in school may depend to a very large extent on the teacher. At this age the child tends to be emotionally involved with her and wants her to like him.

Home and school are now two separate spheres. The child may not like to have his mother walk to school with him or visit school unless it is for a group performance when other mothers are also present. While with the group, the child may ignore his mother.

Seven likes to accumulate school papers in his desk rather than bring them home. Most are interested in a schedule and settle into classroom work with absorption. Both boys and girls are quieter while they work than they were at Six, and talk more to themselves than to others. However, they do refer to the work of a nearby

neighbor, and make impatient demands for the teacher's assistance, often going directly to her desk.

The child of this age is frequently seen with head resting on forearm while writing and while classroom discussions are in progress. He shows temporary fatigue over some tasks by shoving his desk or getting up from his chair. These signs indicate that he is ready to change to a different activity. Energy at this age may be highly fluctuating: It comes and goes. Many children find it difficult to hold up through the customary all-day sessions. Some teachers find that the daily program needs to be flexible in second grade, depending on the fatigue of the students, whereas by third grade the program can remain the same from day to day.

The child of this age can be a serious and sincere student, like the little boy who told his grandmother, "There's so much to be learned." Seven often demands too much of himself and, with his characteristic inability to bring things to termination, often goes on with an activity too long. Then he suddenly collapses. He needs to be helped to define stopping points.

Seven-year-olds have their good days and their bad days, their high learning days and their forgetting-everything days. An aware teacher will shift her intellectual fare on these different days. And a wise mother might even keep her child at home if his bad day starts the minute he gets out of bed, as it often does.

Seven likes to manipulate objects, so he picks up pencils, erasers, sticks, and stones, and accumulates them in his desk. It may be helpful to have a pocket-emptying at the end of the school day, and an occasional desk-cleaning. Seven is apt to pick up things that do not belong to him. This definitely should not be considered stealing. Rather, you can tell the child that when he is a little older he will not need to take things that belong to other people.

Classroom work requires the teacher nearby. There are many individual differences at this age. Some children prefer work at their desk to work presented by the teacher on the blackboard, and vice versa. (Seven does not combine different tasks easily; he finds it very difficult to copy from the blackboard as he sits at his desk.) Boys tend to prefer oral arithmetic to written; girls sometimes prefer the opposite. Some like widely spaced ruled paper; others prefer narrow. Some respond immediately; others need extra time. By Eight there is usually more uniformity within the group.

Seven has a new awareness of endings. "How far shall

I go, Miss L.?" or "I can't finish" are typical remarks. The child likes to complete, but wants the teacher to establish the end for him; otherwise he is apt to continue too long. He likes to have his paper corrected immediately: "Did I get 100?" "Is this right?"

Seven makes a characteristically explosive transition from school room to playground at recess time. On the playground he may be more or less active than in the classroom. Entanglements with classmates occur even with Teacher nearby. One child may interfere with something another is building; one child may want to remain on the swing for the entire period; or somebody may monopolize a ball or jump rope.

When several children attempt group play, they may become excited and hilarious. This usually ends with destruction of material or personal altercation. Seven needs a variety of outdoor equipment, and even though most are not ready for much directed group play, adult supervision is essential.

Seven wants a place in the group and may be concerned that the other children or the teacher do not like him. He can be separated from the group for special help or to work or play by himself, but does not like to be singled out for reprimand or praise while he is part of the group. Group praise, however, is a real spur. The group is slow to include a new member and may at first even make fun of a newcomer. Seven is not a good age for mainstreaming. Children of this age are not too compassionate about those who are different.

It can help a second-grade teacher to succeed with her class if she recognizes such typical Seven-year-old behavior and characteristics as the following:

1. The overall paranoia of the second grade: thinking that Teacher is mean to him, that people will laugh at him, that people don't like him.
2. Overanxiety about being late for school.
3. Extreme dependence on Teacher: inability to start even simple tasks without a special personal word from her.
4. Difficulty in terminating an activity once it is begun.
5. Apparent deafness when given a verbal command.
6. Inability to combine board and desk work, i.e., to copy from the board.
7. Proclivity for taking things—pencils, erasers, or even things that belong to other children—and at the same time, forgetting to take home things that are supposed to be taken home.
8. Expressions of sudden and extreme fatigue.
9. Desire to know the plan of the day—what is going to happen next.
10. A tendency to be highly aware of any mistake he makes. Usually Seven knows when he has failed and wants to do something about it. This may be the reason he erases so much. (Six just ignores mistakes or may mark right over them.)
11. An inability to behave well when Teacher is out of the room.

It is especially important to keep in mind that the typical Seven-year-old is not the expansive, communicative, outgoing person that he was at Six and probably will be at Eight. To a great extent he keeps his thoughts to himself. One teacher we know of, when asked to provide a demonstration of more or less typical classwork, commented that she would demonstrate any class but second grade. Their lack of outgoing spontaneity, in her opinion, makes second graders a poor group for showing off.

If your Seven-year-old is having basic trouble in school, especially with reading and other academic subjects, it is extremely important *before* you undertake remedial work to be as sure as you can be that he actually belongs in second grade and is not overplaced. The Gesell position on school placement is that every child should be started in school, and subsequently promoted, on the basis of behavior age rather than age in years. Many Seven-year-olds, especially if they have fall birthdays, may not be ready for second grade.

When any child has conspicuous difficulty, either in first or second grade, here are some of the questions you can ask yourself. If your answer to most of them is yes, this is a very good clue that your child may indeed be overplaced.

1. Does the child dislike school?
2. Does he complain a great deal that school is too hard?
3. Does the child have great difficulty in completing any written work assigned to the class?
4. Does he seem unduly fatigued when he gets home from school?
5. Is he a "different" child in summer, when school responsibilities are removed?
6. Does he have terrible trouble, almost every day, in getting ready for school?

7. Does he complain of stomachaches, or is he actually sick to his stomach before going to school in the morning?

8. Has any marked change for the worse in health taken place since school started? Does a normally healthy child suddenly begin to have a series of colds, one after another?

9. Have any home routines taken a marked turn for the worse since school started? For instance, does the child eat less, have trouble sleeping, exhibit a return to bed-wetting after having been dry at night?

10. Has a normally "good" child suddenly become rebellious, difficult, quarrelsome, or cranky at home once school has started?

11. Does your child get much worse school marks than you and the teacher think he is capable of getting?

12. Does the teacher assure you that he could do better if only he would try harder?

13. Does your child have trouble socially, either in class or on the playground?

14. Are most or many of the child's friends chosen from a lower grade?

15. Is teething considerably behind that of other children in the class?

16. Does a normally "good" child find it terribly difficult to behave in class? Are there constant complaints from the school that he has had to be reprimanded, was made to sit out in the hall, or had to be sent to the principal's office?

17. Does the child do desperate things at school, such as finish a paper and then scribble all over it?

18. Does the child find it unduly difficult in class to wait his turn, speak only when he's supposed to, refrain from bothering classmates?
19. Does he daydream in class or fail to pay attention to an extent that the teacher considers unreasonable?
20. Has the teacher or anyone suggested to you that your child is not up to the work of the grade?
21. Does your child seem babyish compared to other children of the same age?

One of the best ways to check on overplacement, at this age as well as at others, is to give the child the advantage of a careful behavior test. In our experience the one that has proved most effective is our own.[8]

Several of the subtests that we routinely administer in an effort to determine maturity level, as well as the behavior that may be expected at this particular age, are described below. If your boy or girl is not up to these standards, this may be a clue to unreadiness for second grade.

BEHAVIOR TESTS FOR SEVEN-YEAR-OLDS

PAPER AND PENCIL

Seven shifts both paper and body to the nondominant side when writing. The free hand is relaxed and the child often pins down the upper corner of the paper on the nondominant side with index or middle fingers. His head may be bent way over, even down to the tabletop. The pencil is held tightly, close to the tip.

Now the child can place first and last names at the upper left-hand corner of the paper, possibly crowded at the top. Capitals and small letters are used correctly from now on. The baseline is becoming straight and there tends to be good spacing between the first and second names.

Writing an address is still beyond most Seven-year-olds, but about one-third of the children we tested were able to write the date; nearly all could write the month and year and most could write the day.

COPYING GEOMETRIC FORMS

At this age, children can copy circles, crosses, squares, and triangles without any difficulty. The outside of the divided rectangle is now usually rectangular in shape, and the inside pattern consists of two pairs of lines that cross, though usually not at a central point. This is the first age when the majority of children can copy both the horizontal and the vertical diamonds with reasonable accuracy.

This is also the first time that forms are of an even size for nearly half the children, and are placed in one or more horizontal rows. Most children still use about half a page for the seven forms.

UNDERSTANDING RIGHT AND LEFT AND PARTS OF THE BODY

Fifty percent or more of the Seven-year-olds we tested can name their eyes, eyebrows, palms, elbows, and thumb; 39 percent can give their index fingers some correct name. Thirty percent name middle finger correctly without help; 63 percent can name ring finger correctly. Twenty-eight percent can name little finger, although over half call it "baby" or "pinkie."

Eighty-two percent of girls and 68 percent of boys name their right hands correctly.

ANSWERS TO PERSONAL QUESTIONS

Seven knows not only his age but also the month and day of his birth. He can name siblings and tell their ages.

chapter eight
THE SEVEN-YEAR-OLD BIRTHDAY PARTY

Seven is one of those seemingly inconsistent ages when the child, while having considerable trouble within himself, does not make much trouble for other people. It is frequently the case that at exuberant, outgoing, aggressive ages, such as Four and Six, children are often hard to get along with, but they themselves may not suffer too much because of their own behavior. At the more withdrawn ages, such as Seven, they may give relatively little trouble to others even though they themselves may be uncertain and unhappy. Thus your typical Seven-year-old, although he may at times have difficulty with school or neighborhood friends, can under favorable circumstances be a highly sociable little person.

We find Sevens especially easy to get along with in positive social situations like parties with friends. They may complain before and after the event, but their behavior during a party is often remarkably good. And the control of this age—which may lead to moping, complaining, and sulking at home—seems to help the Seven-year-old to be reasonably restrained and amenable in an outside social situation. Less egocentric and aggressive than Six, less wild than Eight, Seven seems to enjoy tak-

ing part in the kind of group activity that a birthday party provides.

The child of Seven does not always have to win or be first. He not only can take turns but enjoys the notion of turns and likes the idea of having and obeying rules. However, much less exacting and demanding than he will be later on, Seven is not disturbed by moderate infractions of these rules. And so, although behavior can be modified and to some extent governed by the idea of rules, the child does not insist on strict adherence to them to the extent of interfering with a party.

While most Sevens like the idea of rules, they cannot follow instructions that are too complicated. Thus a quick series of relatively simple games works better than a few more difficult activities. Most Seven-year-olds behave well at parties—especially compared with their Six-year-old selves—but you do need to channel their energy and have the timing for the different activities carefully planned.

The Seven-year-old is not a good judge of his own stamina. Sevens in a party situation as elsewhere are given to a somewhat reckless expenditure of energy until they suddenly drop from fatigue. Keeping the party hours brief can prevent this complication.

Seven is somewhat serial-minded and very poor at terminations. It is therefore important to shift quickly from one game to another so that the group will not get "stuck" and go on and on with the same activity until it palls and behavior deteriorates.

In most cases it works out best to have an all-girl or all-boy party. Girls like quieter things, like pin the bow on Ms. Pac-Man or some other timely, newer version of old games. Boys tend to prefer such activities as relay races with a balloon between the knees, and are more concerned than girls about having definite winners who receive prizes.

Although going out to restaurants, ice cream parlors, pizza parlors or video game arcades—many of which now specialize in birthday parties and set aside space for them—is becoming very popular, home parties are still well accepted by most. Parents tend to prefer these because, albeit perhaps harder to give, they are much less expensive. And many Sevens are more comfortable and feel freer to express their natural exuberance in somebody's house rather than in a public place.

Also, if you live in a close knit and competitive neighborhood, you may find it hard to keep up with the kinds of parties "all the other kids" are giving. The following quote is clearly intended as humorous, but it does give an idea of the way things can go.

> Well, so what if Mr. Armando took all the kids up in the Goodyear blimp for Victor's birthday party? Not every party can be totally special. Okay, okay, so Mrs. Anderson took all the kids to Scuba World and they had ice cream on a float in the diving tank. Honey, do I look like an aquanaut? Well, it's just great that Mr. Kroner is a pilot and Billy had his party on a 747 at the airport. But what's wrong with a nice little party in the Happy Room at Burgerland, huh?"[9]

THE SEVEN-YEAR-OLD'S PARTY AT HOME

KEYS TO SUCCESS

This is an easy age for party-giving because most children at Seven are fascinated by the idea of following rules, even though they may not carry them out perfectly.

Number of Guests. Eight is a good number of guests for a Seven-year-old's party, although a particularly effective mother with a helper (another adult is best, but an older sibling will do) might manage as many as ten or twelve. Both boys and girls can be invited, although many prefer to invite just boys or just girls. Girls may not mind too much either way, but many boys definitely prefer just boys.

Number of Adults. Two adults can manage a party at this age: the mother and one helper.

SCHEDULE

From 3:30 to 5:00 is a good time for such a party. One
and a half hours may actually be better than two. Many
become too tired and too excited if the party lasts longer
than this, perhaps because their increasing speed takes
them through so many games.

3:30–3:50　Children will enjoy bingo while waiting
for all to assemble. This is a quiet game in
which they work together. It helps them
get acquainted if necessary, and the number of guests doesn't matter. And children
of this age like working with numbers.

3:50–4:00　Treasure hunt. This can be hunting for
prizes or merely for gum or peanuts.

4:00–4:15　Refreshments. Sevens need a midafternoon
snack, and having refreshments early gives
them the energy to keep going without becoming too cross, hungry, and tired. Refreshments may consist of simple sand-
wiches, ice cream, cake, and milk. Children
at this age tend to approach refreshments
with great enthusiasm but fill up quickly
and soon leave the table. If balloons are
used for decorations, children may start
hitting them and pulling them down. They
may be allowed to do this, but preferably
after eating.

4:15–5:00　A series of games should follow, all at one
level—just game after game for the rest of
the available time. This is preferable to the

large blocks of activity that are appropriate at Six and Eight years. Simple relay games are popular. Other possible games include Musical Chairs, Ring Toss, Pin the Tail on the Donkey, or seasonal variations (such as Nose on Snowman, Hat on Scarecrow).

Prizes are given to the winner or winners of each game. Suitable prizes include paper dolls, toy jewelry, dollhouse furniture, false mustaches or noses, chewing gum, Life Savers, sheets of stickers, Magic Markers, paints, balloons, pencils, models of dinosaurs, *Star Wars* figures, puzzle books, maze books, or dot-to-dot books.

5:00   Ending of party and getting guests home. Children may play games right up to the time the party ends. Then the host's mother takes them home. This gets them out of the house and prevents the confusion that often accompanies parents' arrival. It also saves waiting for the parents to arrive.

HINTS AND WARNINGS

This is an age when chicken pox and other communicable diseases, as well as accidents to arms and legs, may cut down the guest list, so prepare for last-minute replacements.

Some are apt to be very silly at this age. Sevens love to clown, so some clowning should be allowed. It is fairly easy to control. However, behavior is apt to deteriorate unless games follow each other rapidly. All games should be well planned in advance, with all equipment ready.

A party at this age can be very simple, more so than at many other ages. The main thing is to have plenty of games and plenty of prizes, and to have all details ready.

Don't insist too much on strict enforcement of rules. Turns and order are important, but Seven-year-olds do not care about strict adherence to the details of rules. If infractions do indeed bother them, then that is the time to step in. If they are bothered, they will clamor "That's not fair!" Otherwise, don't be too strict. In lining up, children are able to decide among themselves the order. Also, they can usually decide about turns: "I'm first!" The more pushy ones get to be first, but this doesn't seem to do much harm, except perhaps to the adult's sense of fairness.

Have the party in as indestructible a setting as possible. Children will push, jump, scuffle, and knock things over. A basement or playroom setting is good if available.

As at Six, it is important to have paper bags marked with the children's names for their loot, as well as a good safe place where they can put these bags so they won't worry that somebody else is getting their things. Be sure that each child gets at least one prize, even if he doesn't actually win anything. In fact, frequent prize-giving to all is a good plan.

Sevens tend to move as a group. When one does something, the others are likely to follow. A little adult direction is often needed to keep things from getting too far out of hand.

The Seven-year-old party described may sound rather simple and unpretentious, but in our experience it seems to be the way Sevens like it.

chapter nine
INDIVIDUALITY

In order to understand any child, we need to know all we can about three things: his age, what his personality is like, and how he is affected by the environment.

Because we at Gesell put so much emphasis on the way children of different ages may be expected to behave, there are those who believe that we are not interested in environment. This is not the case. Dr. Gesell stated as long ago as the 1940's, "Environmental factors support, inflect, and modify but they do not generate the progressions of development."[10]

There are some who think that Dr. Gesell, unlike Piaget, was not interested in interaction. Actually, Dr. Gesell stated specifically, "Because the interaction is the crux, the distinction between these two sets of determiners should not be drawn too heavily."[11]

Most certainly we need to know all we can about each and every age, and about the way the environment affects the child. But the third factor, individuality, is equally important. The stages of behavior—the way it changes from age to age—are remarkably similar in all children. Environment may be similar or totally different. (That is quite another story, and one we do not attempt to cover in this book.) But whatever the environment, it's safe to say that each and every child goes through the customary stages of behavior in his own individual way.

Here, too, some parents have misinterpreted what Gesell had to say. Because he, and we, provide norms or descriptions of the different stages and ages of behavior, some believe that we think children are all alike. Again, this is not correct. Throughout the Gesell writings one finds the statement that every child is an individual, different in many ways from every other—even from his identical twin. And these individual differences show themselves very early. As Gesell so often remarked, "Even infants are individuals." By the time the child is Seven, he is an individual indeed.

One conspicuous expression of individuality is the rate at which the child goes through the different stages of behavior—how well he fits the norms. We must keep in mind that norms (our descriptions of the ages) are only averages. Some children will fit these norms rather precisely. Some will be ahead. Some, though perfectly normal, will be a little bit behind. When a child is behind (suppose your Seven-year-old is behaving more like a Six-year-old), we say that he is immature. This does not mean that he is dull or unintelligent: There are in fact many bright children who are young for their age. We describe such children as "superior immature" and take great pains to see that they do not start school before they are ready just because they are bright.

A second way in which children of any age differ from one another is the way in which they fit the cycles of equilibrium and disequilibrium, of inwardized and outwardized behavior, described earlier. As these diagrams show, nearly all boys and girls, so far as we have observed them, tend to go through these alternating stages. This we can more or less guarantee. What we cannot guarantee is the place of any child's presumed midline.

Let's say the midline is a bit to the left of the one pictured in our diagram of equilibrium and disequilibrium. (See page 14.) A child with this midline would have—and would give others—an extremely hard time at any stages of disequilibrium; he may not be too easy to deal with even in a stage of equilibrium. As one mother put it, "You said my son would be better when he got to be three, but he was 'good' for only about three weeks."

A child who has trouble with himself and with life tends to go even further than the average into disequilibrium, and things are hard for him and for everyone around him. The opposite, of course, is also true. There are some children so well equilibrated—so comfortable within themselves and with those around them—that even at their worst they do not have, or give, much trouble.

The same is true when it comes to alternating stages of inwardized and outwardized behavior. The terms *introvert* and *extrovert* are in common use. We know that some people, introverts, tend not to be very sociable or outgoing, do not make friends easily, are often quite satisfied with their own company. The typical extrovert, on the other hand, is outgoing, sociable, and gregarious, preferring company and having little wish to be alone.

Thus for the introvert our theoretical midline would be to the left of the "average" one that we have pictured. (See page 15.) The typical midline for the extrovert would be to the right. At Seven years of age, the introvert would go to extremes of pulling in and away from others; the extrovert would remain out there in the social world but might be just a little quieter as compared to his customary self.

There are many ways of thinking about the different kinds of individuality or personality. Since the most effective way we know of is one introduced by William H. Sheldon, we shall describe here, as we did in an earlier volume in this series,[12] Dr. Sheldon's system of constitutional psychology.

According to Sheldon, behavior is to a very large extent a function of structure. That is, regardless of environmental influence—which must of course always be considered—we behave as we do primarily because of the bodies we have inherited. Not only that, but regardless of height or weight or other changes with diet or with age, the basic personality does not change substantially from age to age. Therefore the fact that a person may be overweight or underweight does not change the basic bone structure of his body.

Although nobody is all one thing or the other, there are three main components that make up the human constitution, and in most people one or the other does predominate.

These three components are endomorphy, mesomorphy, and ectomorphy. The body of the endomorph is round and soft; that of the mesomorph hard and square; that of the ectomorph linear, fragile, and delicate.

In the *endomorph,* arms and legs are relatively short compared with the trunk. The upper part of the arm is longer than the lower part. Hands and feet are small and plump. Fingers are short and tapering. In the *mesomorph,* extremities are large and massive, with upper arm and leg equal to lower arm and leg in length. Hands and wrists are large, fingers squarish. In the *ectomorph,* arms

110

and legs are long compared with the body, the lower arm longer than the upper arm. Hands and feet are slender and fragile. The fingertips are pointed.

Recognizing your own child's body type and knowing how endomorphs, mesomorphs, and ectomorphs customarily behave may help you set your own expectations more realistically than might otherwise be the case. It is sometimes easier to understand and accept your child's behavior if you believe that behavior depends to a large extent on the way the body is built.

According to Sheldon, the endomorphic individual is one who attends and exercises *in order to eat.* Eating is the primary pleasure. The mesomorph attends and eats *in order to exercise.* What he likes best is athletic activity and competitive action. The ectomorph, on the other hand, exercises (as little as possible), and eats (with indifference) *in order to attend.* Watching, listening, thinking about things, and being aware are activities most enjoyed.

Another clue to the differences among these three types is that when in trouble the endomorph seeks people, the mesomorph seeks activity, and the ectomorph withdraws and prefers to be alone.

Time orientation may also vary with physical structure. Our experience has been that the endomorph tends to be most interested in the here and now. The mesomorph tends to look toward the future. The ectomorph seems to be the one who is best oriented in time, and shows an interest in the past as well as in the future. He may be the true historian and keeper of diaries.

Now, how do these three different kinds of children behave when they are Seven? We have no word on this from Sheldon, so the following is our own theory. It seems quite likely to us that the plump little Seven-year-old endomorph, at this somewhat negative age, may be expected to slump around disconsolately when things go wrong, stuffing himself with food more than ever when depressed.

The vigorous mesomorph might express feelings that people were unfriendly in a more aggressive manner. This child may become even more aggressively hostile than ever and get into more than the usual number of fights with those who in his opinion are treating him badly.

It seems quite safe to theorize that the Seven-year-old ectomorph will take things hardest, pull away from those cruel others, and withdraw even more tightly than ever into himself. While the mesomorph may express anger and unhappiness by punching somebody out, the ectomorph will express displeasure verbally. Even more than other Sevens, the ectomorph will complain about the meanness, unfairness, and cruelty of other people.

One further aspect of individuality that some investigators set great store by is personality differences due to position in the family. Forer[13] and many others do hold that there are demonstrable and fairly predictable differences between first, second, and third children.

At any rate, it is considered by many that *firstborn children* are achievement oriented and often highly successful in their achievements—in fact are likely to become eminent later on. Even as children they may be capable, strong-willed, and effective. They tend to have a well-developed sense of responsibility, are likely to use words like *should* and *ought,* and want to conform and do things right. They tend to be conscientious in their studies. In fact, their standards for themselves and others are often

extremely high. When they are in the company of others, they like to be leaders. Relationships with parents tend to be close and successful. Firstborns often relate to their parents by developing strong drives of achievement.

Firstborns, perhaps due in part to their usually good relationships with parents and their position of seniority in relation to siblings, often turn out to be secure, self-confident, comfortable, and successful in positions of leadership.

Second or middle children are generally considered to be less highly driven toward accomplishment than their older siblings. They are more spontaneous and easygoing, more tactful, more adaptable, more relaxed, more patient, more emotionally stable, better able to balance opposing forces. They are less likely than firstborns to attain eminent status. A middle child has to learn ways of competing, but *indirect* ways, and so may become rather tricky or even sneaky. Such a child may become a "con man" or may merely learn diplomacy. A second-born may feel that other people make no unusual demands and that he can expect help from others. A middle child may expect an older sibling to look out for him and may be much less competitive than an older sibling, less driven to succeed.

The *youngest child* may feel somewhat inadequate and inferior, more passive and submissive, more accepting of domination, more babyish, less driven toward accomplishment and excellence, more quiet and withdrawn than older children. A youngest child may, even more than a middle child, develop indirect ways of getting what he wants. Failing to do so, this child may either give in or run to adults for support; he is by no means above screaming or tattling. If he never gets his own way, he may become passive and withdraw from others when there is tension and threat in the environment.

In general, however, we do find that third children, especially when they are the youngest in the family, tend to be of a certain sweet and gentle disposition. Many seem to feel very secure in the belief that there will always be somebody older to look out for them. This perhaps diminishes strain and anxiety.

Thus there are really two questions involved here: First, does birth order actually influence behavior; and second, if it does, why is this the case? We cannot give definite answers to either of these questions, but at least they are something to keep in mind as we try to understand the personalities of our children, at Seven or at any other age.

One further aspect of individuality that obviously influences behavior at any age is the child's sexuality. Although some individuals at any age express behavior more characteristic of the opposite sex, we believe that in the majority of cases boys behave in a "masculine" manner and girls are customarily "feminine." Nowadays some environmentalists and ardent feminists insist that there are no innate sexual differences in behavior and that girls and boys would behave just alike if we treated them alike. But common sense and the bulk of observation and research contradict this notion. The most recent report on sex differences in behavior,[14] an extremely interesting and scholarly study of nursery-school boys and girls by Pitcher and Schultz, concludes that:

> children learn narrow sex role concepts which conform in general to their culture's stereotyped belief system. Through their play behavior, children steadily

incorporate the gender role initiated by their biology, demanded by their psyche, understood by their mind, and supported by their culture. Human beings have characteristics which no society has created and to which all societies must respond. Young children acquire a sexual body from their genes, and they develop gender concepts from interaction with the environment. Both are formative influences in the child's becoming a male or female human being.

The authors' observations were that boys' and girls' behaviors differed at each of the ages studied, not only in the roles they adopted, but in the types of behavior favored by one sex or the other. Girls tended to be nurturant, whereas boys favored rough-and-tumble play.

So, Seven or not, don't expect all your children to behave in a similar manner or in the same way every day of the year or in all situations. We once met a very successful (from parents' and school's point of view) Seven-year-old boy whose entire conversation with us during one afternoon had to do with all the accidents he had had or that anyone he knew had had. He also told us about all the bad things that friends and classmates had done: They squirted water, swore, and were unable to spell correctly even such simple but "bad" words as *love*.

In contrast, on a train from Boston to Portland, we met a Seven-year-old girl who told us, "I love school and I love to be in the spotlight. I am the smartest one in school. *I* don't just think so. *Everyone* knows so, except one girl who thinks *she* is as smart as I am. . . ." At the end of the journey she exclaimed, "Oh, here is my wonderful, beautiful Portland. I just love it. I want to thank

you, Louise, for being so interesting and having this nice conversation with me. It made the journey very interesting and I am going to kiss you good-bye."

Clearly a strong sense of self can take one a long way, even through the sometimes swampy terrain of Seven years of age.

chapter ten

STORIES FROM
REAL LIFE

UNHAPPY SEVEN-YEAR-OLD

Dear Dr. Ames:

Can you tell me if I have a real problem with my oldest boy, Seven-year-old Clayton? At Six he was rough, tough, and noisy, but very bright and cheerful and very happy and well adjusted.

He was *so* vigorous that we were much pleased when around the age of Six-and-a-half he calmed down considerably. But now that he has moved on to Seven, he has suddenly become moody and complaining. He acts as if the weight of the world were on his shoulders. He is no longer a happy child.

And ever since he turned Seven he seems to cry at the snap of a finger. He complains that nobody plays with him at school, that he has no friends, that he isn't going to get a good report card.

That is, he complains about things that are happening, things he imagines are happening, and things that *might* happen in the future. His school work has fallen off, and every school morning he complains that he doesn't feel good. His teacher is worried about him, and we wonder if we should worry, too, or if he is just Seven. Do a lot of other children at this age cry and complain at the slightest provocation, or even when there is no provocation?

You've hit the nail on the head. Seven-year-olds normally do cry at any, every, or even no provocation. Seven tends to be a quiet, withdrawn, pensive, and in some even a rather gloomy age—certainly when compared to vigorous, aggressive, demanding Six or expansive, outgoing, ready-for-anything Eight.

Sometimes parents are pleased when their active, noisy, into-everything Six-year-old first starts quieting down and becoming more self-contained and thoughtful. At first it's a pleasure to see your child think before he acts, and you're glad to see him restraining that tendency toward loud, explosive, aggressive behavior.

But as time goes by, many parents begin to wonder if their Seven-year-olds haven't withdrawn too far, become too moody and absorbed with their own concerns. And when the time comes, as it does for many, that tears are followed by more tears, and criticism and complaint become the order of the day, many parents wish they had their noisy little Six-year-olds back again.

The typical Seven revels in his gloom. It's important for parents to realize that the child of this age really seems to enjoy the idea that everyone is picking on him, everyone is criticizing him, everyone is mean to him. Remind yourself of this before you become too critical of the people he accuses.

BOY THINKS THAT EVERYBODY HATES HIM

Dear Dr. Ames:

Will you please help me with a problem that has become so serious that it disrupted our whole household this morning. My son, who is Seven, seems to have developed a "hate" complex and I am at a loss as to how to handle it. He has always been a well-behaved boy, and we have always gotten along fine except for minor skirmishes here and there.

Now all of a sudden all this has changed. He says the children at school hate him; and if I refuse to let him do something, he accuses me, saying, "I hate you and you hate me. You don't love me anymore." This goes on with his father and grandmother also. All we hear is "You hate me and I hate you."

He doesn't even want to go to school now. He is in second grade and is an excellent student. The class chose him secretary of their Red Cross unit and he was quite thrilled by it at the time.

When he told me he wasn't going to school because the kids all hated him, I decided to investigate. My son admitted that only one boy had said he hated him and it turned out to be one of the bullies who all the children are having trouble with.

This morning he stepped on something (or so he said) before putting his shoe on. He came hopping to me and said, "Mommy, my foot hurts awful. I can't go to school." I looked at his foot and could not make out a mark on it. I kidded him about it. Then he changed a little and said it felt better but still he couldn't go to school.

I then tried reverse tactics and said, "All right, if you want to stay at home, it's all right with me." This time he replied, "All right, I'll stay at home and be stupid if you don't want me to go to school and learn anything."

Please tell me, is all this a stage a Seven-year-old boy goes through, or do we have something serious to cope with?

Your son's behavior is typical. It is quite customary for children of this age to think that everybody hates them: their teacher, their parents, their friends, their brothers and sisters. Everybody hates them and is treating them unkindly.

The fact that your son has not acted like this in the past makes us anticipate that in a few months you should have your good-natured little boy back again. If you remind yourself that this behavior occurs mostly because he is at this age, and not because of any real mistreatment he is getting, you can handle this behavior more calmly. Don't take it too seriously and don't worry too much.

Of course you treat it sympathetically. All of this is real enough to him. Continue doing just as you did when he said the children hated him. Talk it over with him and iron things out until he finally has to face the truth that only one boy treated him badly. Work out each situation with him with sympathy and respect. This mistreatment, whether real or fancied, seems very important to him and does make him unhappy.

You have to steer a middle course between feeling sorry for him and not taking his complaints too seriously. If you remain calm but sympathetic and don't let him drag you too far into these confusions, things will go best.

"WE'LL NEVER HAVE A DECENT MEMORIAL DAY"

Dear Dr. Ames:

May I confirm your findings that Seven-year-olds tend to enjoy suffering and worry about almost anything? Our daughter, Cynthia, up till now a reasonably cheerful and happy-go-lucky child, has been incredibly gloomy since she turned Seven. She worries about everything. Just before Christmas she came down with a light case of flu. How she suffered!

She worried that she wouldn't get back to school in time for the Christmas play. She worried that Daddy couldn't afford "all this medicine." And she also worried that Santa Claus (if there is a Santa; she wasn't sure) wouldn't be able to get her presents to her if she was still in bed.

I'm glad that I had already read your warning about Seven-year-olds, or I would really have thought there was something peculiar about our darling daughter.

Thanks. We always enjoy getting anecdotes from parents. I would like to add my own favorite story of Seven-year-old suffering.

I know of a little girl from Maine who was spending the year in Ohio with her graduate-student parents. When Memorial Day came around, she wouldn't come out of her room. She just moped around with the door closed.

Finally, Mother went in and asked her daughter what was the matter. "What's the matter? What's the matter?"

moaned the little girl. "It's Memorial Day and we don't have anybody dead out here in Ohio. We should have stayed in Maine."

And then a look of total despair came over her face. "But we don't have anybody dead in Maine, either. We'll *never* have a decent Memorial Day."

Yes, indeed, your typical Seven-year-old suffers and enjoys the suffering!

GLOOMY THOUGHTS CUSTOMARY AT SEVEN

Dear Dr. Ames:

As I was getting my Seven-year-old daughter, Becky, a cup of water before bedtime, she said to me, "Mommy, sometimes I think you are going to put poison in the water so you can live your own life."

Well, perhaps wrongly, I was shocked and hurt. I said "You must think I'm some kind of witch or something" and left the room, calling my husband to finish putting her to bed. Then I went to my room and cried.

Was I wrong? One minute I think I should have passed it over as her just being Seven. But the next minute I think even a Seven-year-old is old enough to try not to hurt others with what they say.

Becky did cry when I left and said she didn't mean it, but I was too hurt to stay and hear her prayers or kiss good night a child who could accuse me of murder. I felt especially bad because, although I am just a housewife and mother, I have always felt that I was a good, conscientious, loving mother.

I'd say that you did make too much of the whole thing.

Becky actually revealed her age by her thoughts of poison. But because her remark was so dead serious, and it involved you, it was a bit hard to take.

Seven-year-olds are often very liberal with their talk of hating this person and that, killing this one and that one. They like to think about death, killing, poisoning—any sort of violence. (And keep in mind that they don't get these ideas just from radio, television, comic books. Sevens have always enjoyed or been concerned about the horrible—long before we had television.) So Becky's notion about being poisoned is a quite normal though gloomy notion for a child of this age to entertain.

Certainly you couldn't help it if your feelings were hurt. You were probably tired at the time of Becky's bedtime and were quicker to be hurt than you might have been in the daytime.

Our usual advice to parents of Seven-year-olds is to take all this wild talk calmly. We would have told Becky that we most certainly were not going to poison anybody. We might then have gone on to assure her that children sometimes think these things and it's all right to say them, but added that "nobody around this house is going to kill anybody or even harm anybody" or made some other friendly and positive generalization.

Children at Seven have enough trouble within themselves with their violent thoughts without having adults take them seriously.

SEVEN-YEAR-OLD GIRL IRRITATES MOTHER BY DAWDLING AND ANSWERING BACK

Dear Dr. Ames:

My Seven-year-old daughter, Crystal, has lately developed two rather disturbing characteristics. The first is an affinity for doing everything in the slowest possible way. Whether it is dressing in the morning or doing her work at school, she will deliberately take a very long time in getting it done. She dawdles and is easily distracted.

The second thing is an extremely irritating way of answering me back, particularly in front of others. She can be not only deliberately rude but downright impudent. She particularly seems to want to embarrass me when other people are around. These displays of antagonism toward me are infrequent but very embarrassing.

I have tried several methods of dealing with this. I explain and appeal to her innate sense of courtesy—I use incentives—but to no avail. She will cooperate for a while and then lapse into her bad habits again. What do you advise?

Crystal sounds like a Seven-year-old who is still clinging to definite Six-year-old ways. All this seems worse because she is older than Six.

True, there is something very slow and deliberate about Seven. But for all this slowness, most Sevens do get things done. Crystal seems to expend her energies in dawdling. Even though they're slow starters, most

Seven-year-olds can put on a sudden burst of speed when necessary.

How to make things better is quite a problem. Many mothers of Seven-year-olds leave getting ready for school up to the child. Call Crystal in time and see that breakfast and clothes are ready, but let timing be *her* problem. As you take off the pressure, sometimes the child will put more pressure on herself. One or two days of being late for school often speeds things up tremendously.

As for her rudeness, again Crystal seems to have the Six-year-old's uninhibited approach. Many Sevens channel aggression by mumbling or being slightly pert in critical remarks. In trying to overcome Crystal's rudeness, you will have to try to keep discipline as a teacher does. An air of confidence and unruffled calm (which you may not feel) are important. Make her feel that it's going to turn out badly for her if she treats you rudely in public. (Some parents say, "If you must be rude, don't be rude while other people are around.") Crystal must be made to feel that while an occasional outburst may be excused, she just can't get away with being consistently rude.

Your attitude here is important. In helping your daughter to overcome her rudeness to you, it is essential that you realize that even though you're the victim of her rudeness, this isn't necessarily a battle between you and her. Rather, this bad behavior, like any other, is something you can help her conquer by being on her side. Whenever a mother gets emotionally entangled in a battle with her child, she loses her objective ability to help solve the problem at hand.

MOTHER OF DIFFICULT BOY KEEPS AN AT-HOME
REPORT CARD

Dear Dr. Ames:

My Seven-year-old son, Michael, has been a terribly difficult child to live with and almost impossible to discipline.

Mike is attractive, athletic, charming, and a great talker. But he is constantly active, into everything, and seems to have little judgment, inhibition, or self-control. He is my most difficult child and sometimes rather hard to love.

We know that he is the type who, given an inch, will take a mile. He is my challenge and, in many ways, my education. I thought perhaps other mothers might be interested to know of the method that I have used most successfully in the past two years to discipline him.

Since his dad is away much of the time, I've tried keeping what I call a report card—a complete diary of all his activities that don't conform to our family rules. Before my husband comes home on Friday night, I sit down with Mike and go over the notes and ask him if the report is fair.

Seeing things in writing seemed to stun him at first. But it was marvelously effective. He and his dad discussed the report together. After a while, Mike asked if I couldn't put good things in too. At first there weren't too many good things to put in, but gradually the balance shifted.

His dad praised what good things there were, and poor Mike was so eager for there to be more good deeds to add to the report that gradually there were. Good deeds seemed, after a while, to replace many of his most flagrant bad deeds. To date, this has been our most effective method of dealing with this delightful but oh-so-difficult son of ours.

Mike does indeed sound like one of those difficult boys. Fortunately it sometimes seems that mothers of such boys are blessed with special insight and enthusiasm in the business of controlling them.

A report card for a boy like Mike is a splendid idea. Often, physical punishment has almost no effect on such boys as this, and isolation may lead to worse misdeeds. Deprivation makes little impression.

Fortunately these boys often are vulnerable to moral judgments about themselves. (In nursery school we often induce improved behavior by telling them "You bother the other children.") They often have a strong desire to look good in other people's eyes.

Writing down a child's misdeeds may seem like undue emphasis on the negative, but your comment that seeing his bad deeds in writing seemed to stun Mike is very significant. Many of these violent, active little boys do wrong things in the heat of anger, and emotion keeps them from realizing or facing up to what they have done.

While permissive parents all too often tend to avoid facing the realities of their child's behavior, reviewing misdemeanors in cold blood is often the only way some children can be brought to face them. Your kind of handling, which includes both truth and compassion, takes time, effort, and planning. Rearing children is no easy job, but when a successful trail is being blazed, the rewards far outweigh the effort expended.

SEVEN-YEAR-OLD BOY HAS AN EATING PROBLEM

Dear Dr. Ames:

I have a Seven-year-old boy whom my husband describes as an ectomorph. Ever since he was a toddler, he's been a feeding problem. His food likes can almost be counted on one hand. And if I have his favorite things more than once a week, he doesn't like them the second time.

He has a severe nutritional anemia and is being treated for it by our doctor with pills, much rest, and three good meals a day. The latter is the most difficult for me. Big breakfasts are heartily eaten by him if I choose the right foods. But I cannot manage to get two other decent meals into him a day without scolding, bribing, or screaming. I was at the screaming stage tonight and felt so defeated, I had to turn to experts for advice.

Marvin dislikes meat—any shape or form of meat. His main complaint is that he has to chew it. It takes a great deal of mastication for him to get even a chopped egg sandwich down. If he finishes a dinner in half an hour, that's pretty good speed.

Another facet of the problem that worries me is how he feels when I set meals in front of him that he knows he doesn't like or knows will take him ages to chew. He knows he must empty his plate at every meal—doctor's orders—but he still tries to fight it. If I leave him alone, free of any prodding or scolding, he sits for an hour playing with the silverware, his plate untouched.

Is he ever going to hate me because of my insistence

130

that he eat? I want to know if this daily struggle will have any psychological repercussions later on in his life.

I'm so worried about all this that some days I'd like just to dig a hole and crawl in.

We do not like to differ with your pediatrician, but we cannot entirely agree with his prescription. If a child like yours eats one good meal a day, we consider that pretty good. Two would be fine.

Our suggestion would be to give Marvin everything possible at breakfast time, including crispy bacon if you can possibly get him to accept even a sliver. A very light lunch may make it possible for him to eat an acceptable dinner.

Of course, you should be careful to give only the tiniest portions, especially if you are going to insist that your son empty his plate, although we recommend that you give up on that. Just deemphasize quantity. Sometimes these noneaters can get a lot of nourishment from between-meal snacks such as peanuts or carrot sticks. Be sure that things are served attractively; colored cups and plates and pretty napkins sometimes help noneaters.

Hard as it may be to believe, most children do not starve themselves for long. But your emphasis (backed by your doctor) on quantity is clearly killing what little spark of appetite your son may normally feel.

SEVEN-YEAR-OLD SHOWS NO SIGNS OF STAYING DRY AT NIGHT

Dear Dr. Ames:

Our family consists of a girl of Twelve, a boy of Seven, and another little boy age Eighteen months. Our problem is with our husky, active Seven-year-old boy's bed-wetting. For almost five years he has not been allowed any liquids after four P.M. He's been taken to the bathroom at eleven P.M.—although all too often he is already wet—and is taken again at three A.M. All to no avail: He is always drenched by morning. His control is excellent all day, through play and school.

His schoolwork is all A's. He is a top reader in his class, mechanically inclined, always busy and restless. He and his older sister just don't get along. She is very antagonistic and bossy toward him.

We make no issue of his bed-wetting, but he has given up on ever being dry in the morning. When I think that my baby might be trained in the near future while our Seven-year-old is still bed-wetting, I am worried about what reaction it may cause in him. At this stage, having a drink at four P.M. or after has become an obsession with him, and we just haven't the heart to refuse him all the time. Our doctor says we have no problem and has advised against any of the advertised conditioning devices. What can you suggest so that we may give our son some help?

Many normal children are not able to stay dry all night every night until they are Five or Six. So although a wet bed is a nuisance to all concerned, it is really not all that unusual. However, your son is now Seven and it is high time to give him the help he needs.

Withholding liquids after four o'clock often does not do much good and makes life even harder for the child. So we would allow liquids, though not in excessive amounts. And since he is already wet at eleven o'clock and again at three, we certainly would not bother waking him at three. Regardless of your doctor's advice, your best bet is probably to get hold of one of the now generally accepted conditioning devices. They are readily available. There are many different brands, but the device we most favor is U-trol. (See footnote, page 39.)

However, something new has been added to the bed-wetting scene. Although a conditioning device is often your best and quickest solution, physicians have discovered that many bed wetters also have allergies. If the cause of the allergy can be discovered and eliminated, the bed-wetting may stop. In recent years many children have been cured of bed-wetting—and even daytime wetting—by removing milk, wheat, or corn (or in one instance tomatoes) from their diet.

So our advice would be to try a good conditioning device. If it doesn't work at first, put it away and try again in another few months. If this is not successful, find a capable allergist and check to see if your son is allergic to something in his diet. Also check with a competent specialist to rule out a "real" physical problem.

But whatever you do, you probably should not expect a quick solution to this problem. Your son's nighttime pattern of being wet as early as eleven P.M. suggests that it may be quite some time before his body is ready to stay dry all night. You are absolutely right to make no issue of this problem. And since the baby is only eighteen months of age, presumably you have several years to go before his night dryness will complicate your problem.

SEVEN-YEAR-OLD HAS BEDTIME FEARS

Dear Dr. Ames:

All of a sudden my husband and I are having a terrible time with our Seven-year-old daughter, Patty. Patty has never been a really good sleeper but was never too bad.

Now all of a sudden she seems to be overcome with all sorts of night fears. She can't get to sleep and can't stay asleep. In fact, she can hardly bear to be left alone in her room at night. Do you have any ideas on how we can help her not be so afraid and sleep better?

A typical Seven-year-old may be afraid of anything, bedtime included. Our best advice has always been to let the child know that you sympathize with what to her are very real fears but that you are not thrown by them and that life cannot revolve around them.

The child may be afraid of school, but she does have to go. She may be afraid of people, but she does have to meet them on occasion. Bedtime may frighten her, but she does have to go to bed and eventually to sleep.

While many of these fears are temporary and age-related, they are real to the child, and it is friendly and fair to show reasonable sympathy. Therefore, extend your bedtime good-night talking. Some children will at such times tell you what it is they are afraid of. Others can't or won't. Sometimes in these cases, if you start a story about a little girl who was afraid at bedtime, you can get your own child to take turns with you in embellishing the story. It may be easier for a child to talk about an imaginary story character than directly about herself.

Also, try installing a night-light. You can even have a little bell for her to ring if she feels in dire peril, but you have to be careful about this kind of approach, as it can be overused.

In rare instances, a family may even have to call on outside help, i.e., a child specialist, to help them over this Seven-year-old hump. But with most, large doses of homemade sympathy will do the trick.

A rather calm attitude on your part is best. If Patty believes that *you* are really frightened about her fears, then she will be in the soup indeed. So do your best to maintain an even balance between sympathy and calm restraint. We can practically guarantee that a few months' time will see your daughter over this present hurdle.

SHOULD SEVEN-YEAR-OLD WANDER AROUND AT NIGHT?

Dear Dr. Ames:

I read your column faithfully but have never seen a problem quite like ours, if indeed we do have a problem.

Our Seven-and-a-half-year-old boy, Sammy, has started wandering around the house at night. He goes to bed very promptly and falls right to sleep. But recently he has begun waking up a couple of hours later. Usually either a bad dream or the need to go to the bathroom will awaken him. Then he has trouble going back to sleep and roams around his room, sometimes around the whole house, before returning to bed and to sleep.

His father gets very angry about these nocturnal wanderings and has punished him, deprived him of privileges, and ordered him to stay in bed. I think my husband is making too much of this and that Sammy will outgrow this behavior as soon as he finds out what he wants to know.

Sammy's schoolwork is excellent, and the teachers and neighbors like him. He is not a problem boy. He has always been able to handle any of the disturbing situations he has faced (sickness, hospitalization, family moving, etc.). Although he occasionally suffers pangs of jealousy, he is mostly very good with his little brother.

My real question is, are these nightly wanderings and the inability to get back to sleep anything serious? Or are they just a passing phase that he will straighten out by himself if we let him?

Chances are that this nighttime habit of your son's will disappear as quickly as it appeared if you don't make too much of it.

We can understand your husband's feeling that he doesn't like to have the boy do this. But actually your son is doing better than many if he is taking care of his problem himself and doesn't awaken you.

The only reason we might be against this behavior is if you feel he is apt to fall downstairs or otherwise hurt himself. If not, we doubt that it does any real harm. If you prefer, you could insist that after he has gone to the bathroom he go back to his own room. Chances are, since he seems to be a good boy, he will obey this minor restriction. But telling him to remain in bed is not necessary and very likely will not work.

Unless he is doing himself some harm, this is not really a very undesirable or unusual thing for a child to do. No amount of discipline is going to force a child to sleep. And if he can take care of and occupy himself during this wakeful time without making demands of you, you are actually pretty lucky.

YOUNGSTER WHO FIGHTS SLEEP NEEDS PLENTY OF OUTLETS FOR ACTIVITY

Dear Dr. Ames:

Our problem is our Seven-year-old daughter, Lauralee, who is the oldest of our three children. She has always been a very active child who could get by with a minimum of sleep. Many times when she was younger, on the few occasions we traveled by car, rather than lying down to rest she would actually fall asleep on her feet and stand there until her knees buckled.

Lauralee is a very intelligent child: She said her first words at seven months, walked at ten months, and could talk clearly at eighteen months. She's always been quick to learn: At the age of three she drew original pictures that would do credit to a Six-year-old.

We dread the summer and long days, since Lauralee gets up with the sun. Many times in the past we have found her playing in the backyard at five in the morning. In the winter she may sleep until six-thirty. She then wakes up her brothers, who would rather sleep.

We've asked her to go back to bed. We've ordered her to. We've spanked her, talked to her, yelled at her,

and taken her skates, her allowance, and her TV and
other privileges away from her; nothing works. She'll
go back to bed, and when we doze off, she creeps out
of her room again. This goes on six or eight times until
our alarm clock goes off. We ourselves get up fairly
early, so the problem is not that we want to sleep late
(although on weekends we would like to sleep until
eight, just once!).

I'm ready to try anything. We can't continue losing
our sleep as we have in past years. And needless to
say, our patience is at an end.

Is this common in active, rather high-strung children? Do they outgrow it or are they always early
risers? Would some kind of mild sedative help, or is
there another method that we haven't thought of?

This is the kind of problem you sometimes get with a
very active, driven child, the kind who doesn't know
how to stop. However, by the time a child is Seven, you
can usually expect certain things from her, although you
do have to provide outlets for her tremendous round-
the-clock energy.

We hope that Lauralee has a room of her own so that
she does not have to bother her siblings. Can you provide her with an alarm clock that will go off just before
your own? Then she can be allowed to get up and play in
her room, but not go out of the room or bother you until
her alarm goes off, at which time she can come in and
wake you up.

What kinds of planned activities do you have for her
in this early-morning period? Does she have certain special playthings that she plays with only at this time—
such things as puzzles or special coloring books? Do you

leave her special food, such as fruit or crackers, that she can eat when she first gets up?

We are often surprised to note the extent to which a little motivation and planning can calm down a girl like this and keep her from being a real household menace. If all of this doesn't work, is there a relative she can visit for a while, just until you catch up on your sleep? Although we hate to tell you this, some people never need what we consider a "normal" amount of sleep, and your daughter may be one of these people.

CHILD WHO HAS TROUBLE SLEEPING MAY ALSO HAVE A VISUAL PROBLEM

Dear Dr. Ames:

Our Seven-year-old, Patty, is so aggravating that there is little time to be nice to her. Her trouble started last year when she put her arm through our storm door and required twenty-three stitches. After that, she started getting up on the average of five nights a week. I am a nervous wreck from lack of sleep.

I went to a guidance counselor who said that Patty just wanted attention and to give her more in the daytime; then she wouldn't get up at night. However, that didn't work. Then our family doctor found that Patty had pinworms. So we got rid of the worms, but she still gets up almost every night.

When she wakes up in the night, I put her back to bed, and then she asks me to sleep on a cot in her room. I do, but sometimes I sneak back to bed and she doesn't notice. She is better than she was—now she usually wakes only once in the night—so sometimes I really do get a good night's sleep.

My husband says I should just tell her firmly to stay in her own bed and not bother me, but if I do, she screams and wakes up the whole house. I realize, of course, that being a middle child may be the source of her difficulties.

Many middle children sleep right through the night. We doubt that being a middle child is the main cause of Patty's difficulties.

Nor is your husband right when he says you should tell her to stay in her own bed and not come to you. If Patty now awakens only once and will accept being put back to bed—and if after that you can often sneak back to your own bed—you have made a great deal of progress.

We don't always find out exactly what causes these disturbed sleep patterns in children. Sometimes about the best we can do is to help them reach the point where you can all get a good night's sleep. You are on your way.

We are concerned about how Patty had her accident. When a child doesn't see a pane of glass, such as the storm door, we wonder about her vision. Have you checked this? We don't think that Patty wakes up at night just because of her vision, but we do know that difficult children often have many sorts of difficulties. If one of her problems is her vision, this is sometimes a fairly easy problem to solve, at least with help.

See if you can't find a good eye specialist who understands children's vision. You need to find one who understands the difficulty that children's eyes have in focusing in this Six-to-Seven-year-old realm. Surprisingly often, children improve in seemingly unrelated ways once you straighten out their visual problems. At least it's a good place to start.

We suspect that you may have already experienced the worst of Patty's sleeping difficulties. We would anticipate marked improvement by the time she is Eight.

GIRL OVERLY CONSCIOUS OF THE FEEL OF CLOTHES

Dear Dr. Ames:

Have you ever encountered this problem? I have a Seven-year-old daughter, Maria, who is the oldest of three children. She has always been overly conscious of the "feel" of clothes—elastic sleeves, wool, wrinkles in socks, etc. And for the past nine or ten months we have been having great difficulty over shoe-tying. We spend five minutes each morning changing the bow: "It's too loose. . . . Now it's too tight." She is capable of tying them herself, but she says she cannot get them right, and consequently we go through this every day. I do not get angry, but she is well aware that I disapprove.

There is also the matter of her hair. Maria wears her hair in a ponytail and I fix it each day. But after it is done, with every hair in place, she complains that it doesn't feel right and pulls it out, so I must recomb it. Should I go along with this? Her sister is Four, and great competition exists between them for my love and attention. Does this have anything to do with it? Maria seems fairly well adjusted in school and does average or better work.

I would certainly appreciate an analysis of this problem. The reason I don't just refuse to retie the shoe-laces is that, knowing Maria, she would become terrifi-cally upset, and I don't like to put either of us through a screaming session. If I felt one such session would cure it, I would be willing to try; but I'm afraid that each day would be worse, and I don't like to send her off to school all upset.

This may be partly an age problem but seems to be chiefly a personality problem. There are many children like your daughter. Their complaints—that their collars or belts or hair ribbons or shoelaces are too tight, that their braids don't feel right, that their shirts or pants are too tight or are slipping down—seem to result from un-usual sensitivity and real discomfort. Children do not, for the most part, seem to be making these complaints just to get attention, although this may be part of it.

Is there anybody else who can tie her shoelaces for her in the morning—for instance, her father? These children are often most demanding with their mothers, and al-most anybody else has an easier time. Or perhaps you can buy her shoes that don't require lacing?

As for Maria's hair, how about introducing a hairstyle that is less demanding? This may result in some scream-ing and crying on her part, but in the long run it will save everybody a lot of agony.

Such demanding behavior will in all likelihood subside with age. But you may get through the next few months more easily if somebody else takes charge of dressing your daughter. If it's still going to be you, you should try to set a definite pattern of how much help you're going to give with any one problem. Don't try to work this all out in the morning just before your child goes to school:

Any planning should be done at some other time of day.

Once you have made new rules, be firm in carrying them out so that there won't be any loopholes or no room for argument. Many children respond remarkably well to this kind of one-way traffic-handling.

Good behavior should be rewarded. Maria is probably well beyond gold stars. But a trip to the shopping mall with a small amount of money in her hand may relax her inner tensions.

SPANKING DOES NOT SOLVE PROBLEM OF DEEP DISLIKE OF SCHOOL

Dear Dr. Ames:

I am writing to you hoping you can help us to help our Seven-year-old son, Jimmy. For some reason he does not want to go to school. He does his work well, so that isn't the reason. All his teachers have said that he is very shy and that he worries for fear of making a mistake.

The first ten days of school this year went okay until he had a run-in with an older boy. Jimmy then started crying every morning because he did not want to go to school. The principal, the teacher, his father, and I have all assured him this boy will not bother him again, but he still does not want to go to school.

This isn't the first time he has not wanted to go. He had trouble last year too. I have done everything I know. I have pleaded, bribed, and forced him to go. Every day I end up making him go. One day last year and one day this year I spanked him and made him stay in bed all day with nothing to play with, and his father spanked him at night. Several days he has said he would rather have that punishment than go to school.

He also worries over every little thing, not just school. For instance, over the past two weeks he has been afraid that he will get a hole in his underwear. He has never had anything like that happen. Every morning I tell him over and over again that nothing is going to happen to his underwear. I have even bought him new shorts.

His father thinks that if he spanks him every night, that will help. I don't agree. My husband says I spoil him. Jimmy has always eaten a good breakfast and still does on Saturdays and Sundays, but I cannot get him to eat a bite on school days. He says his tummy hurts.

One of his many complaints is that the school day is so long. I have tried having him come home for lunch, but then I have trouble getting him to go back.

Spanking is definitely out. It is not the solution to your problem, and what's more, it is unkind and unfeeling. Your son has a real problem. It is up to you to help him solve it. Punishment is not the answer.

Private school may help. Is there a good one in your neighborhood that you would consider? Some public schools are beginning to realize that younger children need more individual attention and that kindergarteners and first and second graders need to be protected from the older children, especially from the Eight-year-old bullies. Some schools also realize that many children of Five, Six, and Seven thrive better on a half day of school than on school all day. We hope you have such an enlightened school in your town.

Your son's lack of appetite on school days is very telling. This situation obviously bothers him deeply. He is not just pretending. He tells you in no uncertain terms what he wants, what he needs, and what he can stand. It is important to listen to him. With his shyness and requests to stay at home, he is behaving more like a Six-year-old than a Seven. He may do better right now in first grade and by going to school just a half day.

You can hope that he will be tougher in another year and by then won't worry so much.

We do not think you have a severe problem, but we do think that a slight change in the school demands can make your little boy a whole lot happier.

HOW TO TELL A SEVEN-YEAR-OLD BOY THAT HE MUST REPEAT A GRADE

Dear Dr. Ames:

My son Deke will be Seven next October. His teacher feels that he will be much better off in the long run if he repeats first grade. Deke has had a hard time settling down and concentrating, and it is very hard for him to stay in his seat. He has been a problem in class and has been in the lowest first-grade reading group. Apparently he feels that he has to shine somewhere, even if it is only in being the worst boy in the class.

His teacher has been wonderful, but she does feel that Deke is immature and nowhere near ready to go on to second grade. I agree. My problem is how to tell him this without further increasing his feelings of inferiority. Also, how do I keep his older brother, who is jealous of him, from using this as a weapon with which to hurt?

You are to be congratulated that both you and the teacher recognize Deke's unruly behavior for what it probably is: not a sign of badness but an indication that he is too immature for the work and the deportment required of him.

As for how to tell him, your success will depend largely on how you and your husband really feel about repeating. If you feel, as we believe you do, that it is the right thing, the words that you use in telling your son will be less important than your own convincing manner.

Many parents find it works well if they tell the child how lucky it is that they and the school found that everybody made a mistake and started him too soon and expected too much. Point out that he really has done very well under the circumstances, but that the only fair thing to do is to have him repeat a grade so that he can do even better now and in the years to come.

You may say, if it seems necessary to embellish, that people are finding out a lot more about children than they used to know in the past, and now they have found out that boys like him who were not Six until October should really have waited an extra year before going into first grade.

Do not be surprised or too upset if Deke blows up and seems unhappy when he first gets this news. Not all children welcome it, but nearly all will accept it quite cheerfully if they see that you are firm and calm and not upset or angry or disappointed.

As for Deke's older brother, both you and your husband should warn this older boy that there is to be *no* adverse comment—ideally no comment at all. You can threaten severe reprisal if he does say anything. (He may do it, anyway.)

We can assure you that from our point of view you are doing the right thing and that it will pay off handsomely in the years to come.

EPILOGUE

As your child moves on through the primary grades, you will in all likelihood notice that his behavior changes rather markedly from year to year. Of course, major changes do not, as a rule, occur from day to day or even from week to week. But as you look at things in perspective—and this will be the case with many children as they move on through Seven years of age—you are almost certain to note a definite quieting down.

Compared to his loud, active, often aggressive Six-year-old self, Seven tends to be a quiet, thoughtful, sensitive, and even withdrawn person. He is quite touching in his serious approach to life.

If now and then your girl or boy seems to go a bit too far in this seriousness and withdrawal, keep in mind that Eight will bring renewed expansiveness. We often say of Eight that it is an age of speed and expansion. Whichever style of behavior is most attractive to you personally, try to appreciate that nature has her own rhythms and that every age, Seven included, has much about it that is delightful and charming.

APPENDIXES
appendix A

BOOKS FOR
SEVEN-YEAR-OLDS

Aardema, Verma. Bringing the Rain to Kapiti Plain. New York: Dial, 1981.

Alexander, Sue. Witch, Goblin and Sometimes Ghost: Six Read-Alone Stories. New York: Pantheon, 1976.

Ames, Lee J. Draw 50 Dinosaurs and Other Prehistoric Animals. New York: Doubleday, 1977.

Andersen, Hans Christian. The Snow Queen. New York: Dial, 1982.

Baskin, Leonard. Leonard Baskin's Miniature Natural History. New York: Pantheon, 1983.

Berman, Claire G. What Am I Doing in a Stepfamily? New York: Lyle Stuart, 1982.

Bolliger, Max. Noah and the Rainbow: An Ancient Story. New York: Harper & Row, 1972.

Brown, Heywood. The Fifty-first Dragon. Englewood Cliffs, NJ: Prentice-Hall, 1968.

Brown, Marc. Finger Rhymes. New York: Dutton, 1980.

———. Spooky Riddles. New York: Random House, 1983.

Brown, Ruth. A Dark Dark Tale. New York: Dial, 1981.

Carroll, Lewis. JABBERWOCKY. New York: Warne, 1977.

THE CHARLIE BROWN CROSSWORD PUZZLE BOOK. New York: Derrydale/Crown, 1980.

Duvoisin, Roger. SNOWY AND WOODY. New York: Knopf, 1979.

Emberly, Ed. ED EMBERLY'S DRAWING BOOK OF FACES. Boston: Little, Brown, 1975.

Gardner, John C. A CHILD'S BESTIARY. New York: Knopf, 1977.

George, Jean C. THE GRIZZLY BEAR WITH THE GOLDEN EARS. New York: Harper & Row, 1982.

Grollman, Earl A. TALKING ABOUT DEATH: A DIALOGUE BETWEEN PARENT AND CHILD; WITH PARENT'S GUIDE AND RECOMMENDED RESOURCES (new edition). Boston: Beacon Press, 1976.

Hall, Donald. RIDDLE RAT. New York: Warne, 1977.

Hoban, Lillian. MR. PIG AND FAMILY: AN I CAN READ BOOK. New York: Harper & Row, 1980.

————, and Hoban, Phoebe. THE LAZIEST ROBOT IN ZONE ONE: AN I CAN READ BOOK. New York: Harper & Row, 1983.

Keller, Charles. ALEXANDER THE GRAPE: FRUIT AND VEGETABLE JOKES. Englewood Cliffs, NJ: Prentice-Hall, 1982.

————. MORE BALLPOINT BANANAS. Englewood Cliffs, NJ: Prentice-Hall, 1977.

————. NORMA LEE I DON'T KNOCK ON DOORS. Englewood Cliffs, NJ: Prentice-Hall, 1983.

————. SMOKEY THE SHARK: AND OTHER FISHY TALES. Englewood Cliffs, NJ: Prentice-Hall, 1981.

————, and Baker, Richard. THE STAR-SPANGLED BANANA: AND OTHER REVOLUTIONARY RIDDLES. Englewood Cliffs, NJ: Prentice-Hall, 1974.

Kellogg, Steven. TALLYHO, PINKERTON! New York: Dial, 1982.

Kent, Jack. SILLY GOOSE. Englewood Cliffs, NJ: Prentice-Hall, 1983.

Kipling, Rudyard. JUST SO STORIES. New York: Doubleday, 1946.

Lane, Margaret. THE FISH: THE STORY OF THE STICKLEBACK. New York: Dial, 1982.

Levy, Elizabeth. SOMETHING QUEER AT THE HAUNTED SCHOOL. New York: Delacorte, 1982.

Lionni, Leo. CORNELIUS. New York: Pantheon, 1983.

Lorenz, Lee. HUGO AND THE SPACEDOG. Englewood Cliffs, NJ: Prentice-Hall, 1983.

Lubin, Leonard. ALADDIN AND HIS WONDERFUL LAMP. New York: Delacorte, 1982.

Mayle, Peter. WHERE DID I COME FROM? New York: Lyle Stuart, 1973.

McCord, David. THE STAR IN THE PAIL. Boston: Little, Brown, 1975.

Parish, Peggy. NO MORE MONSTERS FOR ME: AN I CAN READ BOOK. New York: Harper & Row, 1981.

THE PEANUTS LAZY DAY DOT-TO-DOT BOOK. New York: Derrydale/Crown, 1980.

Pienkowski, Jan. THE HAUNTED HOUSE. New York: Dutton, 1979.

Pollhamus, Jean B. DINOSAUR DOS AND DON'TS. Englewood Cliffs, NJ: Prentice-Hall, 1975.

Rosen, Winifred. DRAGONS HATE TO BE DISCREET. New York: Knopf, 1978.

Schwartz, Alvin. THERE IS A CARROT IN MY EAR AND OTHER NOODLE TALES. New York: Harper & Row, 1982.

Schweninger, Ann. THE HUNT FOR RABBIT'S GALOSH. New York: Doubleday, 1978.

Silverstein, Shel. THE MISSING PIECE. New York: Harper & Row, 1976.

THE SNOOPY MAZE BOOK. New York: Derrydale/Crown, 1980.

Steinmatz, Leon. CLOCKS IN THE WOODS. New York: Harper & Row, 1979.

Watts, Bernadette. DAVID'S WAITING DAY. Englewood Cliffs, NJ: Prentice-Hall, 1977.

appendix B
BOOKS FOR PARENTS
OF SEVEN-YEAR-OLDS

Ames, Louise Bates. Is Your Child in the Wrong Grade? Flemington, NJ: Modern Learning Press, 1978.

————, and Ilg, Frances L. Your Six-Year-Old: Loving and Defiant. New York: Delacorte, 1979.

————, et al. He Hit Me First. New York: Dembner, 1982.

Bank, Stephen P., and Kahn, Michael D. The Sibling Bond. New York: Basic Books, 1982.

Biber, Barbara, et al. Child Life in School: A Study of a Seven Year Old Group. New York: Dutton, 1942.

Braga, Laurie, and Braga, Joseph. Learning and Growing: A Guide to Child Development. Englewood Cliffs, NJ: Prentice-Hall, 1975.

Calladine, Andrew, and Calladine, Carole. Raising Siblings. New York: Delacorte, 1979.

Comer, James P., and Poussaint, Alvin F. Black Child Care: How to Bring Up a Healthy Black Child in America. New York: Pocket Books, 1980.

Crook, William G. Tracking Down Hidden Food Allergy (second edition). Jackson, TN: Professional Books, 1980.

Delacato, Carl. A New Start for the Child with Reading Problems (revised edition). New York: McKay, 1970.

Dodson, Fitzhugh. How to Discipline with Love. New York: New American Library, 1978.

———. How to Parent. New York: New American Library, 1973.

Ellis, Albert. How to Prevent Your Child from Becoming a Neurotic Adult. New York: Crown, 1966.

Feingold, Ben. Why Your Child Is Hyperactive. New York: Random House, 1974.

Feldman, Ruth D. Whatever Happened to the Quiz Kids? Perils and Profits of Growing Up Gifted. Chicago: Chicago Review Press, 1982.

Forer, Lucille. The Birth Order Factor. New York: McKay, 1976.

Gesell, Arnold, et al. The Child from Five to Ten (revised edition). New York: Harper & Row, 1977.

Ginott, Haim. Between Parent and Child. New York: Avon, 1969.

Graubard, Paul S. Positive Parenthood. New York: New American Library, 1978.

Hautzig, Esther. Life with Working Parents: Practical Hints for Everyday Situations. New York: Macmillan, 1976.

Ilg, Frances L., et al. Child Behavior (revised edition). New York: Harper & Row, 1981.

Jones, Hettie. How to Eat Your ABC's: A Book About Vitamins. New York: Four Winds Press, 1976.

Kohl, Herbert. Growing with Your Children. New York: Bantam, 1981.

Kramer, Rita. In Defense of the Family: Raising Children in America Today. New York: Basic Books, 1983.

Lansky, Vicki. Vicki Lansky's Practical Parenting Tips. Deephaven, MN: Meadowbrook Press, 1982.

Lerman, Saf. Parent Awareness Training: Positive

PARENTING FOR THE 1980's. New York: A&W Publishers, 1980.

Matthews, Sanford J., and Brinley, Maryann B. THROUGH THE MOTHERHOOD HAZE. New York: Doubleday, 1982.

Maynard, Fredell B. GUIDING YOUR CHILD TO A MORE CREATIVE LIFE. New York: Doubleday, 1973.

Pantell, Robert H., et al. TAKING CARE OF YOUR CHILD: A PARENTS' GUIDE TO MEDICAL CARE. New York: Addison-Wesley, 1977.

Postman, Neil. THE DISAPPEARANCE OF CHILDHOOD. New York: Delacorte, 1982.

Rapp, Doris J. ALLERGIES AND THE HYPERACTIVE CHILD. New York: Sovereign Books/Simon & Schuster, 1980.

Schaefer, Charles. HOW TO INFLUENCE CHILDREN: A COMPLETE GUIDE TO BECOMING A BETTER PARENT. New York: Van Nostrand Reinhold, 1982.

Sheldon, William H. VARIETIES OF TEMPERAMENT. New York: Harper & Row, 1944.

Smith, Lendon. FEED YOUR KIDS RIGHT. New York: McGraw-Hill, 1979.

―――. IMPROVING YOUR CHILD'S BEHAVIOR CHEMISTRY. Englewood Cliffs, NJ: Prentice-Hall, 1976.

Smith, Sally L. NO EASY ANSWERS: TEACHING THE LEARNING DISABLED CHILD. Boston: Little, Brown, 1979.

Stevens, Laura J., and Stoner, Rosemary B. HOW TO IMPROVE YOUR CHILD'S BEHAVIOR THROUGH DIET. New York: New American Library, 1981.

Visher, Emily, and Visher, John. HOW TO WIN AS A STEPFAMILY. New York: Dembner, 1982.

Winn, Marie. CHILDREN WITHOUT CHILDHOOD: GROWING UP TOO FAST IN A WORLD OF SEX AND DRUGS. New York: Penguin, 1984.

Young, Milton A. BUTTONS ARE TO PUSH: DEVELOPING YOUR CHILD'S CREATIVITY. New York: Pitman, 1970.

NOTES

1. Herman T. Epstein, report in the BULLETIN OF THE ORTON SOCIETY, Vol. 30 (1980), pp. 46–62.
2. Stephen P. Bank and Michael D. Kahn, THE SIBLING BOND (New York: Basic Books, 1982), p. 198.
3. Albert Ellis, HOW TO PREVENT YOUR CHILD FROM BECOMING A NEUROTIC ADULT (New York: Crown, 1966), pp. 85–90.
4. Paul S. Graubard, POSITIVE PARENTHOOD, (Indianapolis: Bobbs-Merrill, 1977), pp. 31–38.
5. J. S. Chall, STAGES OF READING DEVELOPMENT (New York: McGraw-Hill, 1983), p. 6.
6. Richard A. Hansen and Rebecca Reynolds, CHILD DEVELOPMENT: CONCEPTS, ISSUES AND READINGS (New York: West, 1980), pp. 48–51.
7. Louise Bates Ames, et al., CHILD RORSCHACH RESPONSES, rev. ed. (New York: Brunner/Mazel, 1974), pp. 206–225.
8. Frances L. Ilg, et al., SCHOOL READINESS (New York: Harper & Row, 1978), pp. 23–148.
9. Glenn Collins, HOW TO BE A GUILTY PARENT (New York: Times Books, 1983), p. 62.
10. Arnold Gesell, "The Documentation of Infant Behavior in Relation to Cultural Anthropology," in ANTHROPOLOGICAL SCIENCES, Vol. 2 (1942), pp. 279–291.
11. Arnold Gesell, THE STABILITY OF MENTAL-GROWTH CAREERS (Bloomington, IN: The Public School Publishing Co., 1940), p. 159.

12. Louise Bates Ames and Frances L. Ilg, YOUR FOUR-YEAR-OLD (New York: Delacorte, 1976), pp. 100–107.
13. Lucille Forer, THE BIRTH ORDER FACTOR (New York: McKay, 1976), pp. 45–66.
14. Evelyn G. Pitcher and Lynn H. Schultz, BOYS AND GIRLS AT PLAY: THE DEVELOPMENT OF SEX ROLES. (South Hadley, MA: Bergin & Garvey, 1984), p. 153.

INDEX

• Index •